A Looking-Glass World

FENG JICAI

Translated by
Olivia Milburn

SINOIST

ACA Publishing Ltd
University House
11-13 Lower Grosvenor Place,
London SW1W 0EX, UK
Tel: +44 20 3289 3885
E-mail: info@alaincharlesasia.com
www.alaincharlesasia.com
www.sinoistbooks.com

Beijing Office
Tel: +86(0)10 8472 1250

Author: Feng Jicai
Translator: Olivia Milburn

Published by Sinoist Books (an imprint of ACA Publishing Ltd) in association with People's Literature Publishing House

Original Chinese text © 单筒望远镜 *(Dan Tong Wang Yuan Jing)* 2018, People's Literature Publishing House, Beijing, China

English translation text © 2021 ACA Publishing Ltd, London, UK

ALL RIGHTS RESERVED. NO PART OF THIS PUBLICATION MAY BE REPRODUCED IN MATERIAL FORM, BY ANY MEANS, WHETHER GRAPHIC, ELECTRONIC, MECHANICAL OR OTHER, INCLUDING PHOTOCOPYING OR INFORMATION STORAGE, IN WHOLE OR IN PART, AND MAY NOT BE USED TO PREPARE OTHER PUBLICATIONS WITHOUT WRITTEN PERMISSION FROM THE PUBLISHER.

This novel is entirely a work of fiction. The names, characters and incidents portrayed in it are the work of the author's imagination. Any resemblance to actual persons, living or dead, events or localities is entirely coincidental.

Paperback ISBN: 978-1-83890-513-2
Hardback ISBN: 978-1-83890-514-9
eBook ISBN: 978-1-83890-515-6

A catalogue record for *A Looking-Glass World* is available from the National Bibliographic Service of the British Library.

A LOOKING-GLASS WORLD

FENG JICAI

Translated by
OLIVIA MILBURN

1900

GENGZI YEAR

*The twenty-sixth year
of the reign of the Guangxu
Emperor of the Qing dynasty*

A NOTE FROM THE TRANSLATOR

'Gengzi' or 'Metal Rat' is the name of one year in the sexagenary Chinese Zodiac cycle. In modern Chinese history, a Gengzi year is regarded with particular trepidation due to its eerie tendency to coincide with some colossal disaster.

A NOTE FROM THE AUTHOR

Just as a woman does not seem the same in the eyes of a man as she does in those of a woman, neither does a man appear in the eyes of a woman as he does in those of another man.

Likewise, Westerners do not appear in the eyes of Chinese people as they do in their own; and Chinese people in the eyes of Westerners are nothing like how they seem to themselves.

Today, when someone writes a historical novel, having created their characters they dress them up in historical garb, but they are shown from a contemporary perspective and brought to life by the author's imagination.

PART 1

CHAPTER 1

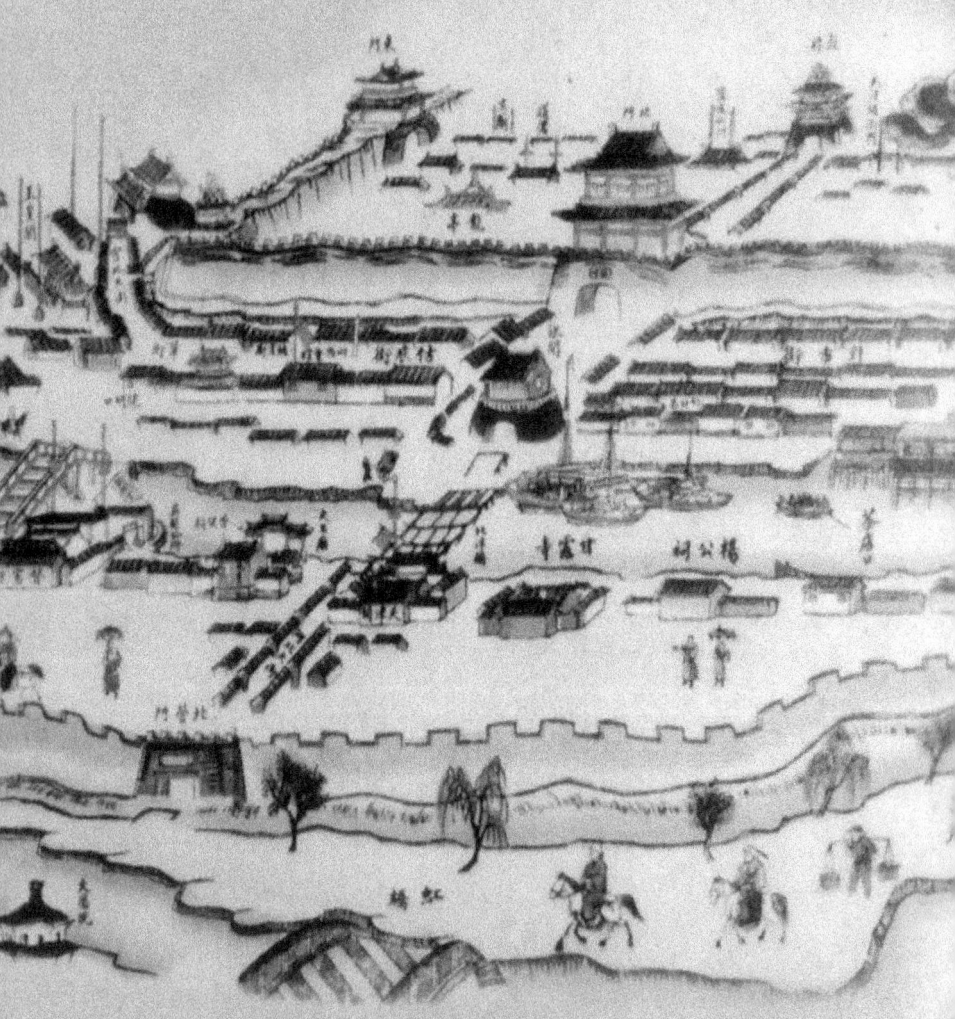

'Map of Tianjin'
A Qing-era woodblock print

ONE HUNDRED YEARS AGO, the house was still here; but one hundred years ago it was destroyed. That means no one alive today has ever seen it.

In those days, in Tianjin, if you hadn't seen this house you really hadn't lived; the same as you were missing out if you'd never heard Liu Gansan singing one of his famous operatic arias or you'd never tasted the Bian family's wonderful crisp-fried fish skin. However, out of all of these things, seeing the house was by far the most important.

People say that when the house was still standing, there was one occasion when a foreigner just stood in front of it and stared. When he had finished admiring it, he raised his camera and then *click*; he'd taken a picture. When other people looked at his photograph, they were amazed too. The house was nothing special in itself: a regular three-courtyard family home. What was remarkable was that a truly enormous scholar tree was growing out of the second courtyard, with a dense crown that covered the house like a huge umbrella. It did not just embrace the middle courtyard but the ones in front and behind as well. What would it be like to live in a house like this? It would be protected from everything by this huge tree – the rain wouldn't wet it, the wind wouldn't blow through it, and it would also be sheltered from the sun. It would be warm in winter and cool in summer, safe and secure. In Tianjin, in the dog days of summer, when every other household had to build a high pinewood scaffolding and hang up thick straw mats to get some shade from the burning sun, this family would not need to do anything of the kind. Their big scholar tree was a natural sunshade – and then how wonderful it would be when it bloomed!

Every May, the whole tree was covered in flowers. At this time of year, it looked like a bizarre bouquet planted in the middle of this large, plain grey-brick house in the northern part of the city: you could see it from miles away. When the wind blew, the unique fragrance of the scholar tree scented the entire district. If an east wind was blowing, the fragrance would be mixed with the scent of burning incense from the City God Temple in the northwestern corner of the walls. If a northwestern wind was blowing, the fragrance of the flowers would mingle with the smell of incense coming from the Buddhist nunnery in the Zhongying area of the city. During the course of the day, the scent given off by the scholar tree was at its most intense in the morning and the evening, which was also when the city gates were opened and closed. The opening and closing of the city gate was done according to the sounding of the bell hung up on the Drum Tower; so the perfume of the scholar tree seemed as one with the rhythmical sound coming from the tower.

Did the scent bring with it the tolling of the bell, or did the tolling of the bell incorporate this special fragrance?

And what about the family living under such a strongly scented tree? How wonderful it must be to breathe this perfumed air, and how soundly they must sleep amid such fragrance! People from the northern part of the city said that whenever a member of that family came out of the house, they brought with them the perfume of these flowers. When the blossoms fell, that was also something to see: the tiles of the roofs and the ground in each of the courtyards were covered in a thick layer of white flowers, like freshly-fallen snow. Sweep it up today, and by tomorrow another layer would have formed. If one of the women of the family stood out in the courtyard for a moment, her jet-black hair would soon be dotted with a few greenish-white or cream-coloured scholar tree blossoms, as if she were wearing jewelled hairpins. It was just at this time that the staff of various old pharmacies from across the city would arrive with sacks to collect the flowers. If a customer went to one of these pharmacies to buy such flowers, the man behind the till would smile and say, "We have scholar tree flowers from Master Ouyang's house over on Fushu Street!"

Old Master Ouyang was very proud of the fact that his family always had such high-quality blossoms.

When the flowers started to fall, he particularly enjoyed putting out an empty teacup on the stone table in the middle of the courtyard. He would pour plain boiling water into the cup, adding nothing else at all, and then he would wait. Sooner or later, some blossoms from his scholar tree would float silently into the cup. Once they started to steep in the hot water, the petals would unfurl one by one, and then his cup of fresh and fragrant scholar-tree tea would be ready to drink...

It was at once magical and yet completely ordinary.

Did such a house really exist? Why did it disappear? Where did the family go? What about the huge old scholar tree? It is not like you can just move an enormous tree like that! Didn't you say that a foreigner took a picture of the house? Where is it now? I'm afraid even those who have seen the photograph wouldn't necessarily understand the story behind it.

But why insist upon seeing the photograph? It is just a picture, after all... how long can it last? If you want to know what really happened, you will have to read what comes next.

When it comes right down to it, I have no idea how old this house actually was. As I have already explained, one hundred years ago it was destroyed, but its history goes back much, much further.

Some people claimed it was built as early as the Ming dynasty, while others said it was constructed by a merchant in the Salt Gabelle in the early Qing dynasty. The thing is that nobody could quite be sure. Anyway, later on, the merchant moved away, and after the house changed hands several times it was redecorated and renovated by successive owners until there wasn't much left of the original Ming dynasty fabric. All that survived were the pair of stone tigers guarding the main gate, which still bared their teeth aggressively: they looked very much in the Ming style.

A house will always reflect the character of its owners: whoever is in charge will make his mark, the same way that the country can be transformed in the hands of its emperor. Only the old scholar tree in the second courtyard remained unchanged, since nothing short of death would move it from its place. Right at the end of the nineteenth century, a scholar pointed out that since ancient times we have built houses first and then planted trees. We don't plant trees and then build the houses around them. So if we knew how old the big scholar tree was, we would know how old the house was. Then an expert on trees stood up and proclaimed that this scholar tree had to be at least three hundred years old. In that case, the house could also be dated to the reign of the Wanli Emperor of the Ming dynasty. However, that would just mean that it was first constructed in the reign of the Wanli Emperor. From the gatehouse to the murals on the wall, they were all added later. In the reign of the Daoguang Emperor, the owner of the house had got rich overnight selling imported goods, and in true nouveau-riche style, he'd had the place done over with extra gold leaf on everything, in the hope of blinding his visitors with his money. Originally, he'd wanted to completely demolish all the old buildings and reconstruct from scratch on new foundations six feet higher than the old ones, paving the whole place inside and out in freshly polished stone. Fortunately, his wife didn't like the fact that so many birds nested in the old scholar tree and their sticky droppings fell on you whenever you went in or out, so the man changed his mind and bought a large plot of land out on Hebei Liangdian Street, behind the Hebei grain store, built a new house there, and moved away.

The old house had been very lucky: this time it escaped destruction.

When the house was bought by Old Master Ouyang, who had just arrived from Cixi in Zhejiang Province to open a paper shop in Tianjin, it experienced a transformation. Old Master Ouyang knew exactly what end was up. He fell in love with the house, and he particularly admired the elegance and simplicity of its construction, that quality which only old, well-built buildings have: he appreciated the fineness of the brickwork, the beautiful mossy window-frames, and most of all the startling spectacle provided by the ancient scholar tree.

Although Old Master Ouyang was a businessman, like so many merchants from Zhejiang, he was also something of a scholar. People from the two provinces of the Yangtze River delta – Jiangsu and Zhejiang – have long been famous for their love of learning. The difference is that Jiangsu people are amateurs of calligraphy and art, so poets and painters are everywhere. Zhejiang people are either officials or merchants. When they finish their education, half of them go on to become bureaucrats, and the rest go into business. Even a little place like Old Master Ouyang's hometown, Cixi, had produced more than five hundred scholars to pass the civil service examinations in the course of its history. Anyway, Zhejiang has always been noted for civil rather than military officials, and its businessmen are Confucian merchants. Although they may make plenty of money, they don't lack for books at home. So Old Master Ouyang didn't exactly renovate his house, but he certainly made sure that all of the tacky decor was replaced. He removed the strings-of-cash and money-bags themed stone or wooden carvings and replaced them with pastoral scenes; musical instruments or calligraphy; plum blossoms, orchids, bamboo and chrysanthemums; or depictions of the Eight Immortals. What he was doing was getting rid of the ugly and vulgar gloss that a succession of owners had added, restoring the old house to its original simplicity and elegance. He understood that by this time, the grace of the Ming dynasty original had been utterly lost, but the more of the old fabric he could leave untouched, the better it would be.

Old Master Ouyang was the head of the household, so by rights he should have lived in the innermost courtyard. However, the two back courtyards were so shaded by the old scholar tree that little sunshine made its way through. The old master liked his flowers, so he lived in the front courtyard. Here there was sunshine in the morning and evening, which is the best light for certain kinds of plants.

On entering the first courtyard, it was dappled with shade. The main hall had originally been intended for entertaining guests, so the ceilings were very high, and the doors and windows were big, making it feel open and airy. One day, as Old Master Ouyang was sitting in the hall, he noticed that the shadows of the branches falling across the ground looked like an ink painting; it really was quite beautiful. His favourite poet was Su Shi, so this naturally put him in mind of the line "The shades of the scholar tree fill the hall" from his 'Epitaph on the Hall of Three Scholar Trees'. It struck him as a very apt description of his own courtyard, so he went to the trouble of asking Zhao Yuanli, a famous calligrapher from Tianjin, to write out an inscription for him: "Shades of the Scholar Tree Hall". Afterwards, he spent a lot of money on having Zhu Xinglian, the city's most famous woodcarver, cut these words into a hardwood plaque. The ground behind the inscriptions was painted, and the characters themselves were gilded, and when it was hung up right in the middle of the wall facing the entrance to the hall, it looked very elegant and refined; it was the epitome of what he was trying to do with the whole house. Because he was so happy with what he had achieved so far, he decided to add an ornamental gate to this hall's entrance. The carpenter came especially all the way from the old master's hometown of Cixi, and it was done in a very plain style, with no paintwork or anything, just the natural colour of the wood, pure and simple in its elegance. Again, there was an element of nostalgia in how he chose to do this.

Old Master Ouyang's wife had died when he was still living back in his hometown. When he moved north to Tianjin, he did not find the women there at all compatible, so he had decided to remain a widower. Now his two sons had both grown up and had families of their own. His eldest son was Ouyang Zun; the younger Ouyang Jue.

Ouyang Jue lived in the third and final courtyard. The branches and leaves of the huge old scholar tree were at their densest to the north, so this courtyard got very little sun, particularly in the summer. In the years before he got married, every day when he had his siesta there would be a little patch of sunshine, about the size of a book, that shone down through a gap in the canopy and in through the window: it would warm his chin – an odd but also curiously comfortable sensation. Sometimes he was even reluctant to get up, for fear that the sunshine would somehow disappear. Indeed, in the year that he got married, the leaves on that part of the tree suddenly put on a spurt of growth, and the gap was gone. His bedroom never got the sun any more, and this made it danker and gloomier than before. He was young then, and very healthy, so he barely noticed this; he certainly did not realise that it would mark the beginning of all his troubles.

The Ouyang family had now lived in this house for more than twenty years. Old Master Ouyang was always very proud of his magnificent scholar tree with its enormous trunk free from any holes, knots or burrs – this tree also never attracted insects. Tianjin stands on land reclaimed from the sea. The water here is brackish, the soil alkaline, so you cannot grow pines or cypresses, only scholar trees and willows. The riverbanks are lined with willows, and on dry land you find the scholar trees. The old city had existed for five hundred years at this point, and most of the old trees inside the city were in the northern half; everyone said this had something to do with the quality of the water flowing through the Grand Canal as it looped past the northern walls. But somehow, in the late Qing dynasty, these old trees started to wither and die, one after the other. Apart from the black locust tree in the Jin family's One Hectare Garden, which was struck by lightning one night leaving it looking like a blackened pole, none of these trees had so much as got sick. Then, for no reason at all, they just seemed to turn yellow and sere until one day they were dead. It was is if they were dying of old age. Every time one of these ancient trees was lost, the people who had lived beneath it were upset for a long time. But there was no point in being sad – the dead trees weren't going to come back to life. Nevertheless, there was a strong sense that things in the city were going wrong. Some people said that ever since the foreign devils had fought their way over the walls during the Second Opium War back in 1860, things were not right in Tianjin. The foreign devils had never left, after all. Instead, they were now living permanently in the Foreign Concession in Zizhulin, and there was a lot of construction going on as they spread their tentacles further and further.

However, other people would then ask if that was the case then why was the Ouyang family's old scholar tree still as flourishing as ever, standing there all by itself, blooming away year after year, spreading its perfume to thousands of houses, and shielding the old house as it had always done? Furthermore, wasn't the Ouyang family's paper business just as successful as it had ever been?

Well, sooner or later all good things come to an end. At the beginning of summer in the twenty-fifth year of the reign of Emperor Guangxu, the scholar tree started to flower and then something strange happened. The old tree, which had never suffered the slightest insect damage before, was suddenly coated in what the local people called 'hanged-man' caterpillars. Long, fine filaments hung from the tree, and on the end of each one was a fat, wriggling green caterpillar. This was the first time that any of the Ouyang family had ever seen this disgusting kind of creature, but before they could think of a way to deal with them, the whole place was overrun.

There were hundreds, and then thousands, of these 'hanged-man' caterpillars which seemed to have appeared from nowhere: they were everywhere in the house, lying dead on the ground, crawling all over the place, wriggling about and apparently trying to tie themselves in knots. When walking through the courtyards, with every step the long filaments hanging from the tree would attach themselves to you, sticking to your face and the soles of your shoes, while the ground itself was slick with the slime of dead caterpillars. One day, one of these 'hanged-man' caterpillars attached itself to Ouyang Zun's wife's neck and then slipped inside her collar. At the best of times, Wei Xifeng was the kind of person to make a mountain out of a molehill, and now she screamed like a stuck pig. She asked the maid, Mrs Jiang, to reach her hand in and get it out. When she was finally able to extract the horrible little thing, she threw it onto the ground and stamped on it. The whole family was kept fully occupied for days using every method they could think of to get rid of these terrible creatures, and afterwards they scrubbed clean all the floors, stone tables and benches, railings, the well-head and every single pair of shoes they owned. After more than a month of labour, having finally got rid of them and feeling that they could enjoy some peace at last, all of a sudden a murder of crows moved in.

There had always been crows living in the city, but you did not often get to see them. There weren't that many of them; you might see two or three at most. Now here were twenty or thirty of them, a huge group, cawing ceaselessly like women quarrelling. These crows were black and huge: nobody had ever seen such enormous crows before. They were the size of cats, and their cawing was truly ear-splitting. Everyone thought they would leave after a few days, but apparently they didn't have the slightest intention of going anywhere. Every evening at dusk, they would gather on the tree, in larger and larger numbers. As soon as they arrived, all the other birds vanished – they were probably scared away.

Then it was autumn, and the leaves began to fall. Between the dense branches, you could see dark shapes: these were the crows.

The more leaves fell, the clearer you could see them. Some people said that they got so fat by eating beggars' corpses out of the open pits over on the west side of the city. At dusk, they would fly into the city and spend the night on the Ouyang family's big scholar tree. Standing on the northern city walls, some people had seen them flying in formation as the sun set, circling and cawing aggressively as they did so. Why had these scavengers suddenly decided that they wanted to stay the night here? Were they going to cause trouble?

Old Master Ouyang was unhappy because he thought it was a bad omen.

One day, Old Master Ouyang raised his head and spotted a big crow's nest in the crook of a branch right up near the top of the tree. It was bigger than a suitcase. He was not pleased to discover they were planning to settle down. If creatures with such disgusting habits started living right above their heads, the *fengshui* of the house would be ruined. Old Master Ouyang hurriedly instructed his servant, Qian Zhong, to knock it down with a pole. However, the crow's nest was too high in the tree: even if they tied three bamboo poles end to end, it would not have been long enough to get at it. Therefore, the servant got out a ladder and used it to climb up into the tree. Unfortunately, Qian Zhong was too old for this sort of thing: his feet and legs were not limber enough, so he missed his footing and fell, breaking his bones. It was so painful that he came out in a sweat. Old Master Ouyang made haste to call in the best bonesetter in the city, Wang Shi'er. After prodding him a bit, Wang Shi'er pronounced it a serious injury since he'd broken his hip. For anyone over the age of sixty, a broken hip is about the worst kind of injury that you can have because it very rarely heals properly, so many people are crippled afterwards.

Qian Zhong was an old servant who'd come with Old Master Ouyang from his hometown twenty years ago. He was not only a trusted servant, careful and clever, but was also able to cook proper Ningbonese food. People from Ningbo have delicate palates and cannot easily get used to the coarse meat-and-two-veg kind of food that Tianjin people like to eat. Tianjin people just gulp their food down like hungry tigers, while Ningbo people eat like birds, picking here and there. Now to have Qian Zhong hurt like this felt like losing an arm. Old Master Ouyang arranged for the staff in his paper shop to send Qian Zhong back to Cixi to recuperate and hire another manservant to take his place. The man they found for him was called Zhang Yi, and he was in his forties. His forehead was shaved, the rest of his hair being gathered into a queue at the back, and he had huge hands and feet. He was obviously hale and hearty, just what you would expect from a native of Tianjin. Old Master Ouyang was quite pleased with Zhang Yi since he was a warm and friendly character, and loyal to boot. If the job called for physical strength, he wasn't the type to hang back. The only problem was that you had to tell him exactly what to do and what not to do; he just wasn't as quick on the uptake as Qian Zhong had been. However, it does not do to make invidious comparisons. In the future, cooking would have to be entrusted to the housekeeper, Mrs Jiang. She was a Tianjin local too, but she was a considerate and careful type – having worked so many years for the Ouyang family, she'd learned a lot from Qian Zhong about how the Ningbonese like things to be done. Having made these arrangements, Old Master Ouyang felt that he would be as comfortable as possible under the circumstances.

Their troubles were far from over, however. On New Year's Eve, Zhang Yi suggested to Old Master Ouyang that he ought to be setting off firecrackers to blow away the bad luck of the past year – this was the custom in Tianjin. Old Master Ouyang agreed and bought a whole load of firecrackers. Who would have imagined that the fireworks would end up setting fire to the tree? When the fire broke out, the flames roared up into the sky in a brilliant blaze. You would have thought that the whole house was just about to go up in flames. They were very lucky that not far away there was a charitable fire-brigade. Summoned to the scene by the beating of a gong, they arrived almost immediately and set to work with a will, four copper-spouted fire hoses dousing the flames simultaneously. The fire was put out before it could spread to the house, but a large part of the tree was burned away. Where the branches and leaves had once grown densely, there was now just empty space through which you could see the sky, and what is more, this burned patch was just where the old master could see it when he was sitting in his living room. Old Master Ouyang was not happy, looking at this empty spot. It felt as though a window had fallen out of the wall, leaving the house open to the four winds.

"Don't you feel that something just isn't right?" Old Master Ouyang asked with a wry smile.

His family tried to cheer him up by saying that when spring came, the tree would be putting out new leaves and new branches, so gradually it would grow back.

But when spring came the following year, the big scholar tree was forgotten because something strange was happening all over the city of Tianjin. The streets were full of people who'd come in from other provinces. They looked like farmers, but they were dressed in a most peculiar manner. Some of them had a red or a yellow bag suspended from their belt, while others wore turbans on their heads, but it wasn't a Taoist turban, nor yet a soldier's one. Where did these people come from? Why were they here?

One day, a fat man with dark skin came in through the East Gate, walking down the middle of the road. When he met the traffic head-on, he didn't move aside; it was the carts and carriages that had to move to the side of the road, as if he were the local magistrate or something. He had a round, fleshy, rubicund face and only one eye, with which he glared aggressively at everyone. His head was wrapped in a yellow turban, embroidered with a pattern of 'Kan' symbols – the sign of the Eight Trigrams that pertains to the north – done in red thread. When he passed the Taotai's yamen opposite the Temple to the Maitreya Buddha, he grabbed a lump of sticky glutinous rice-cake from the stall nearby, went over to the yamen, smeared it on the wall next to the entrance, and then *bam* he slapped a yellow poster up. The poster was covered in text and pictures: the text written in black ink and the pictures done in red. When people went over to have a look, they could read the first two lines up top: "The Northern Six Districts Iron Cloth Kungfu Experts Can Halt the Winds and the Flames. Sacred Warriors on their Battle Steeds: Let the Eight Trigrams Assemble." The rest might be pictures or magical talismans, but no one could make head nor tail of them. When they turned round to look for the fat dark-skinned man, he had vanished without a trace.

On hearing about this, Old Master Ouyang couldn't help connecting these events with the evil happenings in his own home over the course of the last six months or so. He felt uneasy, and his heart began to thump. Afterwards, he would kowtow a few extra times in front of his household shrine every day, silently praying that everything would be all right.

CHAPTER 2

Inside the Temple of the Queen of Heaven

THIS MORNING, the second young master, Ouyang Jue, was feeling very happy as he came out of the house under the old scholar tree. There was nothing specific to make him happy, but young people are often cheerful for no particular reason.

It seemed as though spring – new life – was pulsating through the tree. The aged, blackened branches of the ancient scholar tree were putting forth new shoots. These shoots looked almost like little beans: plump and green, bursting with life.

Ouyang Jue was wearing a long blue robe and a waistcoat edged with velvet piping. On his head, he wore a black silk skull-cap, and his face beneath it was pale, with red lips and white teeth. His eyes shone like stars. The trinkets dangling from his belt were all fine antiques... in fact, he was dressed like any of the other young masters of good family in the city. He walked out of the northern district and bought three pieces of Manchurian candy with assorted fillings in the Tolling Bell Gardens by the Drum Tower, unwrapping them one by one as he walked, popping them in his mouth and chewing them with evident enjoyment. Swinging his arms, he headed straight down the main avenue leading to the East Gate. By the time he passed the East Gate, he had eaten all three of his candies. However, even though there were lots of stalls selling savoury and sweet snacks in and around the gate, he wasn't going to buy any of them. Naturally, he didn't eat that kind of rubbish.

Inside and outside the walls of Tianjin were two different worlds. Most of the rich people lived inside the walls, which was also where the yamen and government offices were located. The vagrants, petty criminals and poor day labourers mostly lived outside the city. You could see exactly who you were dealing with from the way they were dressed: people living inside the city wore robes, with waistcoats or long coats according to season, while those from outside the walls were dressed in trousers and a vest. It is easy enough to understand why – a vest is perfect for someone engaged in hard physical labour.

In those days, the Tianjin city wall was on its last legs. Many of the grey bricks lining the pounded-earth core had fallen off. Through every dynasty, it had been necessary to repair the wall and replace any bricks that had been lost. But in recent decades, the government had been perennially short of funds. Just like the poor who can't afford to keep their teeth in good repair, everyone living inside the walls just had to get used to the growing gaps. In this way, the city wall got more and more dilapidated until it was quite frankly falling apart: weeds appeared in the cracks between the bricks, and there were even small trees growing in some places where sections were missing. There were wild birds building a nest on the forked branch of an elm tree here. Ever since the city had fallen to enemy forces during the Second Opium War, they often forgot to close the gates to the city overnight, and the waters in the moat had turned black and stagnant, stinking to high heaven.

There were plenty of idlers and coolies crowded around the barbican to the East Gate; some of them were unemployed, while others were there hoping to pick up a day's work. This kind of place attracts all sorts of people, and there were plenty of criminals among them, which ensured a constant tumult. Ouyang Jue's appearance and exquisite get-up might easily have attracted unwelcome attention. Therefore, he speeded up and walked swiftly over the pontoon bridge across the moat, and from Mopan Street he turned west onto Gongnan Avenue. With another few steps, he spotted the eye-catching sign of the family paper shop off in the distance. The Ouyang family owned two large paper shops in Tianjin, under the brand name 'Broadlight'. One was on Guyi Street outside the North City, and the other was right there on Gongnan Avenue, next to the Jade Beauties store, famous for its artificial silk flowers. Diagonally opposite was Tianjin's main temple dedicated to the Queen of Heaven.

Old Master Ouyang was the owner of the two branches of the 'Broadlight' paper shop. He was in his fifties, which is to say that he was not old at all, and still very strong. But two years ago, on leaving the Guyi Street branch, he had slipped on the rain-slicked street that had recently been repaved in slate slabs. Just one misstep, and there he was, lying on his back like a beetle. He was very lucky not to have broken anything, but he tore any number of ligaments and muscles: he said himself that he felt as though he had been run through a wringer. Afterwards, he bought himself a top-quality purple bamboo walking stick to help him stay mobile, and the eldest young master, Ouyang Zun, was put in charge of the business.

Ouyang Zun was seven years older than Ouyang Jue, and the two brothers had totally different temperaments. The eldest young master was a typical shrewd Zhejiang businessman – an old head on young shoulders. He was very practical, careful with his money and kept a close eye on trade. At home, he was rather henpecked, but when it came to his business dealings he always came out on top. By comparison, Ouyang Jue, the second young master, was much more scholarly. He spent all his time writing poetry and practising his calligraphy and painting. Although his father and elder brother were active in the business, he had nothing to do with it.

Tianjin was and is a port city, a centre for the import and export trade. Here, ink was used for keeping accounts, so the second young master's lovely calligraphy was quite frankly useless. Everyone said that the Ouyang family had two young masters: one to make money and the other to spend it. Fortunately, neither of them had the slightest interest in whoring or gambling, nor were they endlessly caught up in little schemes and scams, so they got along perfectly well together and never quarrelled. Ouyang Jue was highly intelligent but naïve. However, he trusted his elder brother in everything and admired him enormously. Ouyang Zun was sure to protect his younger brother through thick and thin, and both of them were obedient to their father. As a result, this family had never been the subject of gossip or salacious rumour – you just had to respect them. Old Master Ouyang was very pleased with how things had turned out.

In those days, the Ouyang family owned what was the best paper shop in all of Tianjin. They stocked every kind of paper that you could imagine, bought in straight from the manufacturers. They got their Xuan rice-paper direct from Jing County; their parchment from Wenzhou; their bamboo paper from central Hunan; and their sutra paper was always sourced from Fuyang. At that time, Tianjin people had translucent paper pasted up in the windows instead of glass, and they used 'blind pattern' Koryŏ paper for this, which was shipped directly from Korea. As for all the various kinds of new and popular foreign papers, the eldest young master organised that with the people in the Foreign Concession, and they came to Tianjin from overseas. Tianjin had not only a seaport but also good connections with companies all over the world, which meant that the foreign papers for sale in shops in Beiping, Baoding, Ji'nan and so on were bought wholesale from the Broadlight. Who else could supply them, if not the Broadlight? The eldest young master had a knack for spotting new business opportunities, and he was not the kind of person to let them slip through his fingers. If it was something to do with the trade in paper, and he could see a profit in it for himself, he would go for it. Whether it was woodblock-printed stationery from the Studio of Refined Beauty marketed at students, or Yi Deyuan's tracing paper for marking embroidery patterns that was bought by women, or even blank papers for folding fans ready to be painted, they were all held on consignment. This attracted customers to the shop day after day.

The elder young master said that the worst thing for anyone in business is to see their shop empty. The emptier it gets, the fewer people come in; while if it is packed, everyone else is determined to crowd in too.

Every good businessman has his own secrets for success.

Today, as soon as Ouyang Jue came through the door to the shop, even though his brother was nowhere in sight, he called out, "Where did you put the set with the twenty-four flowers that you were keeping for me?" He was talking about a new run of stationery produced by the Studio of Refined Beauty, with multi-colour woodblock prints of flower springs designed for them by Zhang He'an. These letter papers were absolutely exquisite, as fine as anything put out by the Studio of Glorious Treasures in Beijing, and the customers were ripping them off the shelves just as fast as the staff could stack them.

He looked around for his elder brother. There were a couple of people standing by the counter over on the left side of the room, and when he called out, they turned their heads. He was stunned because one of the faces looking at him was of a strange, exotic beauty – a foreign woman!

He had never seen a face like that before: her skin was like the pale and delicate petals of the lotus flower, faintly suffused with a blush, and her sapphire-blue eyes sparkled and shone. The ringlets escaping from beneath her wide-brimmed hat were like golden waves, and her skirt was puffed out like a cloud… He was standing some distance away from her, which was why he had not noticed her presence to begin with, but he had no idea whether he was indeed looking at a great beauty, or whether she struck him that way because he had never seen a foreign woman before. He just stood there and gaped.

Now he heard his brother's voice. "Let me introduce you. This is Mr Ma, who has come from the Foreign Concession to help us with importing the foreign papers we need. Oh, of course, you've met… you know each other. This is Mademoiselle Xénia, who has only recently arrived from France. She's living in the concession here in Tianjin. Mr Ma has been showing her the sights today."

Ouyang Jue was still feeling a little confused. He had no idea what to say, so he kept repeating, "Too kind, too kind…" Given that this was all he had to say, nobody was quite sure what he meant. The foreign woman could not understand a word of what he was saying, so she kept looking at Mr Ma, as if she were expecting him to translate. Mr Ma had no idea what he should do.

Ouyang Jue realised that he had just said something stupid. He didn't know why he had been so silly, and he blushed hotly. He didn't know what to say next.

Mr Ma was no fool. He knew how to smooth things over and immediately changed the subject with a view to glossing over this momentary embarrassment. "I was just about to ask the elder young master where you were," he said with a smile, "but here you are…" Then he continued, "This isn't just Mademoiselle Xénia's first visit to Tianjin, but it's also her first trip to China. As soon as we turned into Gongnan Avenue, she decided that she loved the place, so I was thinking of taking her around the Temple to the Queen of Heaven. I am sure she'd enjoy it." After that, he tried to teach Ouyang Jue and Xénia to pronounce each other's names.

Ouyang Jue got 'Xénia' right straight away, but she simply could not pronounce the name 'Ouyang Jue' correctly. Try as she might, she could not wrap her tongue around it, and her enunciation was all over the place, but she kept on wanting to say it properly.

Ouyang Zun, who was standing to one side listening to this, said with a smile, "I know she's trying to say 'Ouyang Jue', but it sounds to me like 'Ow-my-jaw'!" That made everyone laugh.

Xénia saw that everyone was laughing but didn't understand what it meant. Mr Ma translated the joke for her, and she laughed too, pointing at Ouyang Jue and giggling, "Ow-my-jaw!"

Now, Ouyang Jue started laughing too. The feeling of constraint was gone, and all of a sudden it felt like they were old friends. He was happy to be friends with her.

Ouyang Jue was surprised at just how easy it was to get to know this young French woman. Why wasn't she shy and retiring like Chinese women?

After a little more conversation, the eldest young master said to Mr Ma, "The Temple to the Queen of Heaven is right opposite us. My little brother knows the place well, so why don't you ask him to show Mademoiselle Xénia around?"

The eldest young master was trying to clear the shop of people who weren't going to buy anything. However, when Mademoiselle Xénia was made aware of his suggestion, she was absolutely delighted. She seemed to be interested in getting to know the young and handsome 'Ow-my-jaw' better.

The idea also pleased Ouyang Jue. He escorted the pair of them out of the paper shop.

Ouyang Jue had never been shopping or sightseeing with any woman other than his wife, and certainly never with a foreign woman. At that time, foreigners were rare, and when they appeared, they were treated as if they were in some kind of peep show. Today, he too was the cynosure of all eyes. Walking along the street, everyone was staring at them. At that time, many Tianjin residents were still afraid of foreigners and would try to avoid them. They would look at them from a safe distance, or they would be pointing their fingers behind their backs. This foreign woman obviously could not care less what other people thought about her; she was intent on having fun and expressing her own opinion on matters. As to what she was saying, Ouyang Jue did not understand a word. However, Gongnan Avenue was the oldest shopping street in Tianjin, and everyone knew that the Temple to the Queen of Heaven was built long before the city was even founded, so the best food and the greatest fun was always to be had right here on this street. Xénia's sapphire-blue eyes kept darting back and forth, but she seemed hardly able to take it all in. She wanted to know about what other passers-by were wearing, what they were holding and what snacks they were eating – she was curious about everything, particularly the women's feet. The tiny feet of women from wealthy households were hidden beneath their skirts, but women from poorer families wore either short dresses or trousers, revealing their bound feet as they tottered along. The foreign woman with her unbound feet was so shocked her eyes were popping, and she pointed at the Chinese women's feet as she asked one question after another. It was so blatant that the women on the street simply fled to avoid her.

Xénia was full of questions for Mr Ma, though sometimes she wanted to ask Ouyang Jue something and needed him to translate for her. No matter how clearly he explained, Xénia didn't understand. Sometimes, Ouyang Jue tried to speak a few words directly to her, but Xénia just shook her head and smiled, shrugging her shoulders – he was speaking Chinese, and she didn't understand what he said. When she smiled, she looked even prettier.

Xénia was entranced by the main hall of the Temple to the Queen of Heaven. Each of the statues on the altar was famous for its spiritual powers, and Xénia was fascinated to hear the stories told of them. When she caught sight of the Daoist Goddess of Vision, with eyes all over her body, she was so surprised that she cried out. Ouyang Jue got Mr Ma to explain to her that the goddess was responsible for curing people's eye diseases. In return, Xénia told him in the West there was a deity with eyes on the palm of its hand, which could see into the future. Ouyang Jue was not quite sure what the point of "seeing into the future" might be.

However, Xénia was still unclear about how the lady with all the eyes could possibly help cure people of ocular diseases. She had her own ideas about the role of this deity. "Surely the eyes all over her body means that she can see everything – the past, the present and the future?"

They seemed to be at cross-purposes in their conversation. At that moment, they both started to wonder whether the problem lay with Mr Ma being quite useless as an interpreter.

Now Ouyang Jue had a good idea. He led Xénia up a steep and narrow staircase to Zhang Xian's Pavilion in the northeast corner of the Temple to the Queen of Heaven. Since the tutelary deity, Zhang Xian, was deeply respected by local women as the protector of infants and children, the tiny pavilion dedicated to him was packed with worshippers from morning until night. Ouyang Jue took Xénia there not because he wanted her to admire the statue of the god drawing his bow to shoot down the Heavenly Dog as it threatened to engulf the sun but because from the windows of the pavilion you could get a panoramic view of the whole temple: the open square in front, the theatre, and the bustling crowds moving up and down Gongnan Avenue. Looking further, you could see the vast sweep of the White River, and beyond that, far in the distance, the strange towers and pinnacles of the Foreign Concession in Zizhulin. This vista made Xénia almost speechless with excitement.

They stood side by side, leaning against the window. He pointed here and there, telling her that this was the stage where operas were performed during the temple festival, and those two tall flagpoles had once been the masts of ships. Over there, the rows of small glittering white hillocks along the river were the saltworks, and if she looked even further east, she could see where she lived in Tianjin – the Foreign Concession at Zizhulin.

Suddenly, Xénia seemed to think of something. She took a six-inch-long bronze tube out of her handbag. This bronze tube was beautifully finished in black leather. She twisted it back and forth in her hands, pulling out each section one by one, until it was quite two feet long. This object was widest at the front and narrowest at the back, and both ends were fitted with thick glass lenses. She raised it to eye-level and then pressed the thin end against her right eye-socket while pointing straight ahead with the thick end. Ouyang Jue was most curious: what on earth could this thing possibly be? Before he could ask, Mr Ma explained, "Foreigners use these things in battle, you know. You can see things far in the distance really clearly."

"Is that what they call 'an all-seeing eye'?" Ouyang Jue asked. "I've heard about them, but I've never seen one before."

"This is what foreigners call a telescope," Mr Ma said. "They have monoculars and binoculars, depending on whether you look with one eye or two. Let me tell you something about telescopes: I could be standing ten miles away, and if you looked through one of them, you could still pick me out from a crowd!"

"Then it really is like an all-seeing eye," Ouyang Jue said. "Isn't that amazing?"

Mr Ma didn't offer any further explanations but translated for Xénia what he had just said.

Xénia was clearly interested in what he had said, and when she heard Mr Ma's explanation she immediately turned round and handed him the telescope with a smile. When Ouyang Jue took hold of it, he held it up just as Xénia had done, but when he looked through the lens, everything was blurred. "I can't see a thing!" he exclaimed.

Mr Ma had no idea why he couldn't see anything.

It was Xénia who spotted that he was holding the telescope the wrong way round and looking through the large end. She burst out laughing, and her laughter made everyone within earshot turn around. Xénia quickly worked out a way to teach him how to use the telescope properly. She pointed it at one of the boats on the White River, and having got the focus right she told Mr Ma to get him to look at the boat. When Ouyang Jue picked up the telescope, this time there was an "oh" of amazement: he really felt like he possessed the all-seeing eye of one of the Four Heavenly Kings! He could even see the beard, the tobacco pouch and the eyes of the old boatman standing by the prow – it was just as if he were standing straight in front of him. He marvelled at the almost magical powers of this foreign object. Xénia reached out, and now she aimed the telescope at his paper shop on Gongnan Avenue. It so happened that Ouyang Zun was just at that moment escorting a customer out of the door. He could see the small mole on his brother's chin so clearly that he felt that he could almost reach out and touch it.

Xénia was very happy. She was enjoying giving Ouyang Jue a new experience. He had shown her round the temple and allowed her to enjoy many novel and interesting things, and this was her opportunity to pay him back.

They had both had a wonderful time, but now Xénia had to go home.

They had travelled from the Zizhulin Foreign Concession in a horse-drawn carriage, which even now was waiting at the entrance to Gongnan Avenue. He escorted them to the corner; but when Xénia and Mr Ma got into the carriage, Ouyang Jue suddenly felt as if he had lost something. He had never felt that way before and could not explain his emotion. Maybe it was just his imagination.

That night, the whole family ate dinner together. Ouyang Jue was sitting at the table next to his wife, Zhuang Shuxian, and suddenly she turned to him and said, "What is that perfume? I've never smelled anything like it."

"It must be the scholar tree," Ouyang Jue said with a smile. "However, it is still far too early for that to be flowering. I can't imagine what this scent is that you are talking about..." As he said that, he gave a start: could it be Xénia's perfume? When they had been leaning against the window together at Zhang Xian's Pavilion, looking out with her all-seeing eye, he'd noticed that she smelled delicious, and the scent she used was particularly delightful. Had he somehow or other managed to get her perfume onto himself?

He gave such a start that the morsel of fish held in his chopsticks dropped onto the table. The eldest young master realised that something was up, and he immediately changed the subject. "I know what that fragrance is. This afternoon when he came round to the shop, we had some scented notepaper out on the counter, just in from the Foreign Concession. I really don't think we can keep things like that in stock because if we aren't careful, all our calligraphy and drawing papers will end up scented too."

Old Master Ouyang smiled. "We have a lot of paper for calligraphy and drawing – a scholar's study really shouldn't smell like a boudoir."

Everyone laughed and carried on eating.

Since it was nothing, naturally the moment passed.

CHAPTER 3

A family photograph dating from the late Qing dynasty

OUYANG JUE HAD no idea how his wife, Shuxian, could have smelled another woman's perfume on his body. That night, when he took off his robe, he sniffed at it, but no matter how hard he tried, he couldn't smell anything different. The odd thing was that when he got up and dressed the next morning, he could then smell the strange perfume that Xénia had worn the day before. The moment he noticed it, his heart skipped a beat: was this some kind of magic?

What particularly confused him was that his wife also used a scented face-powder every day, but he'd never really noticed it, nor had it permeated his very body.

Did foreigners use scented face-powder too?

For many days, he wore the same robe so that he could enjoy her perfume when he dressed each morning. Did he really like that fragrance so much? Or was it the fact that the moment he smelled that scent, it immediately reminded him of her beautiful and exotic face, her strange crystal-blue eyes, and her voice saying "Ow-my-jaw"? Then one morning as he crawled out of bed, he couldn't find his robe anywhere; it turned out that Shuxian had given it to Mrs Jiang to wash.

Shuxian was curious and said, "You've been wearing this robe for seven or eight days now, and the collar is filthy. Why don't you change it?"

After washing, the fragrance disappeared, and it seemed to him as though there was something missing from his life. Ouyang Jue had now become a regular visitor to the shop on Gongnan Avenue. His brother told him, "If there's something you need then let me know. I can bring it home for you. There's no need for you to keep coming round in person." He was afraid that his elder brother might see that something was up: he was very sharp. After that conversation, whenever he went to Gongnan Avenue, he would deliberately avoid the paper shop, walking twice round the place before heading back. It was pointless though; the foreign woman never appeared, and he became more and more despondent. One day, he thought to himself: She's seen all the sights there are to see around here, so why would she come back? He felt a little silly. It was as if some rare bird had been blown off course, had come to perch on his arm for a moment, and had then flown away again.

Once he thought about it like that, he started to calm down and went back to his old pursuits: visiting friends and practising his calligraphy.

Other people might imagine that as a good businessman himself, Old Master Ouyang would favour the elder of his two sons. His eldest son was clever and hardworking, and had done very well for himself. He had already taken over the management of the family business – their two paper shops – and he was making money hand over fist. However, if anything, he loved his "idle layabout" of a younger son just as much. Every time someone praised Ouyang Jue's extraordinary literary talent, every time they mentioned how his poetry, calligraphy and painting were considered among the finest in Tianjin, Old Master Ouyang would smile so widely that his eyes vanished into a pair of crescent moons. If his younger son had no head for business, it was good to see him become a famous artist. Besides which, it was not as though the family needed him to work. The two paper shops were coining money. Of course, although the Ouyang family was wealthy, they were not to be compared to the eight main families in Tianjin who held huge fortunes.

Scholarly and studious Zhejiang people tend to have their feet on the ground; they do not like to be too ostentatious and boastful. They want their lives to be stable, with sufficient money that they don't have to worry. Every year on the first day of the fourth lunar month, when the festival to the City God was held, the richest families in the city would all set up a tented area at the entrance to their homes to show off whatever masterpieces of calligraphy and paintings they owned. Old Master Ouyang, on the other hand, would simply place a Ming-dynasty-style red lacquer altar to the left side of the gate, and on top of it he would position a gilded wooden statue of the thousand-arm Guanyin, Goddess of Mercy, which had been carved at Dongyang in Zhejiang Province. It was an exquisite piece, very old, and looked wonderful sitting on the altar, wreathed in incense smoke. He asked Ouyang Jue to write a calligraphic inscription on red paper, reading, "Her Numinous Spirit Appears Above Us." This was hung up overhead, and when passers-by saw it they would all kneel down and pray.

In a port city, nobody can escape censure. Some people said that this old Zhejiang geezer was sharp as a knife. He put Guanyin in front of his house because he wanted people to have to kowtow to his family. But who would have the gall to tell him to take it away? Even Tianjin gangsters, ready to smash up the houses of even the most powerful and rich families, wouldn't dare touch a Guanyin. They wouldn't want the goddess sending a few thunderbolts down after them, now would they?

Old Master Ouyang had heard plenty of gossip on the subject, but he didn't say a word. Every year, when the festival to the City God rolled round, he would still put his Guanyin out in front of the door. In recent years, the displays set up by other big families had been the site of robberies and muggings, but the Ouyangs living under the old scholar tree were safe and sound.

It all goes to show that educated people have the right idea about how to do things.

Old Master Ouyang loved his younger son very much, not just because he was so clever and diligent, but also because of his innate kindness. Old Master Ouyang had no daughter, but his younger son's obedience and thoughtfulness made up for this deficiency. Ouyang Jue had never made his father angry – in fact, he was afraid of his father's anger. He always wanted to make him happy. Whenever he was out and about and happened to see some fresh flowers for sale on a stall, he would buy them to brighten his father's courtyard. When his father fell and injured himself so badly that he ended up having to walk with a stick, knowing how much Old Master Ouyang admired the Song dynasty scholar Su Shi, he wrote out his line "My bamboo cane and straw sandals make for a pleasant walk" and had someone engrave it on his father's purple bamboo walking stick. Having this line from Su Shi's poem carved onto the stick was intended to be an auspicious message for him. His father was absolutely delighted with it and often showed it off to others.

Old Master Ouyang also cherished his younger son for the sake of his deceased wife. He and his wife had been very much in love, but men must endure their going hence, even as their coming hither – they have no say at all in matters of life and death. His wife had died in childbirth, and the baby she left behind was Ouyang Jue. Just before she died, his wife's last words to Old Master Ouyang were, "If you don't treat him well, I will curse you from the Underworld." This was why he had never married again. Their son symbolised the love and affection he and his late wife had for each other.

When Ouyang Jue grew up, his father had gone to a lot of trouble to find him a suitable wife, finally settling upon a short, plump and good-tempered daughter of the Zhuang family. Although quite pretty, she lacked vivacity, with small facial features, and only single-fold eyelids. Other people said that all he cared about was the Zhuang family money. They were big players in the silk industry, owning the oldest and biggest emporium in Tianjin. The profits of selling paper are as nothing to those from selling silk, since a ream of paper is worth less than a foot of silk. Everyone thought that the Ouyang family was damn lucky to be able to marry a Miss Zhuang.

Vulgar people use money as a measure of success, so naturally they would not be able to understand why Old Master Ouyang would pick such an ordinary girl for his son. He chose her not just because she was so sweet-natured, gentle and patient but also because she was a studious little thing and would have something to talk to her husband about. He was also pleased because the Zhuang family traced their ancestry back to Qufu in Shandong Province, the hometown of Confucius, so he felt confidence in the moral qualities of his son's bride. There weren't many girls like her in Tianjin. He wasn't thinking about showing his daughter-in-law off to other people; he wanted her and his son to be able to live happily together. So he found a reputable friend from the city to act as a matchmaker, and everything was soon settled with the Zhuang family.

No matter what other people said about him, within six months of the wedding, everyone was deeply impressed by how sensible Old Master Ouyang's choice had been. The bride might not have much to say for herself, but she was very kind and got along well with the rest of the family. When she was talking with other people, the moment the slightest quarrel arose, she would immediately change the subject. To begin with, they all thought that she was just being cautious, but gradually they realised this was what she was like – she was not in the least bit quarrelsome or competitive. She went through life calmly; and although she was not a quick worker, she was seldom idle. Sometimes when the servants were hard at work on tasks like cleaning the house and courtyards, scrubbing and sweeping and tidying up, she would take a hand. It seemed that she could not tolerate the slightest speck of dust or any disorder in the house. She would even clean the inkstone on the second young master's desk. Once, Ouyang Jue said to her, "Don't touch the ink on my inkstone because I like to use it after it has rested for a while." She didn't say a word but just smiled. After that, she never cleaned the inkstone again. She would just put the cover straight if the second young master had left it askew.

The second young master spent half of his time in his study and the rest of his time in the studios of his friends. He didn't talk much with his wife, and this made people think that perhaps they didn't get on too well together. One day, when Old Master Ouyang was chatting with his son, he happened to ask, "What do you and Shuxian like to talk about?"

"We discuss all kinds of things," Ouyang Jue said with a smile. "She doesn't say much, but she likes to listen to me." This was very reassuring for Old Master Ouyang.

On another occasion, Old Master Ouyang heard Mrs Jiang mention that since the second young master liked eating melon seeds, whenever she had nothing better to do, Zhuang Shuxian would peel them for him and put them aside in a small white porcelain jar. Every day, that little jar would be placed in readiness on the second young master's bookcase. Mrs Jiang smiled and said, "When the second young master is working away at his calligraphy or painting, he can eat a whole jarful of melon seeds in a couple of handfuls."

When he heard this, Old Master Ouyang smiled so widely that his eyes disappeared into little curved slits. "Shuxian spoils him," he said. After that, he was quite sure that his son and daughter-in-law were happy in their marriage and there was nothing at all to worry about.

However, as time went by, he realised that there was a source of concern here. Not only did his second daughter-in-law show no sign of getting pregnant, but his eldest son's wife also had no children, and she and Ouyang Zun had been married for more than four years.

To have no children after getting married is a big deal for a woman.

Ouyang Zun's wife, Wei Xifeng, was a completely different kind of person from Zhuang Shuxian. Their temperaments were diametrically opposed. One was quick, and the other was slow; one was impatient, and the other gentle; one wanted her own way in everything, while the other was for peace at any price; one was quarrelsome, and the other was placid; one was picky about food, and the other ate whatever was put in front of her; one wore heavy makeup, and the other hardly any; one was always dressed in the most eye-catching bright colours, while the other wore only elegant and dignified shades; one was out shopping every day, while the other hardly ever set foot outside her home; one was talkative, and the other silent; one never read a book, while the other was happiest when reading; one came stamping along as she walked, while the other never made a sound as she moved from place to place. But the two women were identical in the strange and annoying problem they were both having with getting pregnant.

Wei Xifeng started to get anxious when she had been married for three months without becoming pregnant. Over the past few years, this had become a bigger and bigger issue for her. She went all over the place to consult wise women and famous doctors, taking every kind of medicine and strange concoction, but none of it seemed to make the slightest difference.

If a Tianjin woman wants to have a baby, she goes to the Temple to the Queen of Heaven to 'tie a child'. Xifeng dragged Mrs Jiang off to accompany her to the main hall of the temple, where she prostrated herself to kowtow to the Maiden Who Brings Children. According to the rules of 'tying a child', when the goddess is not looking – in fact, the goddess was a clay statue, so how could she be looking – you should 'steal' one of the three-inch-high little child figurines from under the Queen of Heaven's throne. Then, you take it back home and hide it in a cupboard somewhere where nobody else will see it.

This figurine represented the child that the Queen of Heaven would give you. Although it was made of clay, you had to take care of it. At meal times, you should put some food in front of the figurine, and make as if you were feeding it. Everyone agreed that the clay figurine would only work if you treated it properly. If you didn't conceive that first year, you had to go back to the temple to burn incense and kowtow, and then beg the Queen of Heaven for a baby all over again. You also had to take your clay figurine with you, and it would go back to the workshop to be reshaped. Once recast, it would be a little bigger, since a year-old baby would be bigger too. If one day you did indeed get pregnant and give birth to a child, you didn't need to return your clay figurine to the temple. Instead, it was referred to as 'Elder Brother' and kept in your family shrine at home. This was because it was sent by the Queen of Heaven to bring you your baby and would keep your child healthy and happy forever.

Once Xifeng 'tied' a figurine at the Temple to the Queen of Heaven, she looked after it as if her life depended on it. One day, not long after she first brought it home, she suddenly started throwing up all over the place and was quite sure that all this rigmarole had worked. Then the doctor came, and it turned out she wasn't expecting after all. She had always been greedy and was endlessly snacking, and she'd turned her stomach by eating too many dried apricots. She'd been so happy, but it turned out to be nothing at all. This humiliation made her all the more quarrelsome, and she put the entire blame for her childlessness on the eldest young master, screaming and shouting at him all the time. She made so much fuss that even complete strangers had heard all about how useless he was in bed. The eldest young master was afraid of her, so he had to suffer this treatment in silence.

But now there were two childless daughters-in-law, so how was she going to explain that? What on earth could be the matter?

Zhuang Shuxian was always very level-headed and unemotional, so she was hardly going to discuss her private affairs with anyone else. Nobody would dare to question her on the subject, and when Xifeng tried to hint things, all that happened was that the corners of her mouth lifted in a gentle smile. She gave no indication of being anxious, nor was she rushing around demanding medical assistance. When she returned to her parents' home over in the west part of the city, she might perhaps have whispered something to her mother, but nobody could be sure. However, Old Master Ouyang had noticed that occasionally a faint melancholy would drift across her face like a cloud on the surface of a calm lake.

In those days, it was treated almost as a crime for a young woman to get married and then not to have children for her husband's family. One day, Wei Xifeng was quarrelling with the eldest young master, shouting about one thing after another until she got round to the topic of why she didn't have any children. Then she bellowed at the top of her voice, "And who's to blame for this? Why can't Shuxian get pregnant either? It is all the fault of your house being so damn dark! The *fengshui* is completely ruined by the big scholar tree. You can't even grow grass in this courtyard, so how can you possibly expect me to give birth to a baby! You dig out that tree, and that'll be an end to it!" Xifeng's voice now rose to a screech.

Old Master Ouyang was sitting in his living room, and he could hear Xifeng screaming in the next courtyard loud and clear. Although he said nothing, he was not happy. The way she put things was so unpleasant, so aggressive, she might easily offend someone badly. After all, can a tree live to be hundreds of years old without acquiring some numinous powers? As things transpired, he was right to be concerned.

Xifeng had her screaming fit at the beginning of summer. Not long afterwards, the 'hanged-man' caterpillars suddenly appeared from nowhere. After that, the crows took over, and then their old servant, Qian Zhong, fell and broke his hip. Then on New Year's Eve, the firecrackers burned a chunk out of the big tree. Where once he could have said with the poem, "The shades of the scholar tree fill the hall", there was now a glaring brightness as the sun beat down. It seemed as though their good days were coming to an end, and there was nothing that anyone could do about it... and he had no idea what to expect next.

One day, the elder young master sent someone home to find Ouyang Jue and tell him to go over to the shop on Gongnan Avenue. The messenger didn't know what this was all about; he just said that the sooner he went there, the better.

As Ouyang Jue sped down Gongnan Avenue, far in the distance he could see two people standing in the entrance to the Broadlight paper shop: one of them was his elder brother, Ouyang Zun, and the other he didn't recognise – he was standing there smoking a cigarette. Cigarettes were imported from overseas; unlike the dry-leaf pipe tobacco that Chinese people kept in pouches, this foreign shredded tobacco was pressed into thin paper tubes and then packed into paper packages. People would tuck these packets into their pockets, and when they wanted to smoke they would take out a cigarette and light it with a match – so much more convenient! There is also a special fragrance to this shredded tobacco, so once you got used to it, you would never go back to the pipe again.

Ouyang Jue was well aware of the fact that paper shops are terrified beyond anything of fire, so you were not allowed to smoke inside. Anyone who wanted to smoke had to go outside. As he got closer, the man puffing away at his cigarette turned out to be Mr Ma. He was amazed and went over to chat to him. "What are you doing here?"

Most unexpectedly, Mr Ma grinned and said, "I'm here to collect you, aren't I?"

"What do you want to collect me for?" Ouyang Jue asked.

Mr Ma was still smiling. "It's not me that wants to see you – it's that French girl that you took round the Temple to the Queen of Heaven, Mademoiselle Xénia."

Ouyang Jue felt his heart singing, and he couldn't help asking, "Why does she want to see me?"

It was more than a month since the first time they'd met. To begin with, he had thought that it was the start of a real friendship, but then later on he'd come to the conclusion that it was only a chance encounter and put it out of his mind. He had no idea that she still remembered him and had gone to the trouble of asking someone to go and seek him out.

"Mademoiselle Xénia said that you're a good person," Mr Ma

explained, "and she likes you very much. She said that she had a lovely time when you showed her round the temple, and ever since then she's been talking over and over about wanting to invite you to visit her at home. However, I've been so busy that it's only today that I've had time to come here."

Ouyang Jue was surprised. "She wants me to go to the Foreign Concession? When?"

"It's been difficult for me to make it out here even this time," Mr Ma said, "so if you're not otherwise occupied, how about we go now? I've already told her that if I found you here today, I'd be sure to bring you back with me."

Ouyang Zun, the eldest young master, was standing off to one side. He found the whole situation quite bizarre and was not at all sure how to deal with it. He cracked a joke with Mr Ma. "We don't want this foreign woman leading my little brother astray! Otherwise my wretched sister-in-law will be throwing herself down the well one of these days."

"You shouldn't say anything so inauspicious!" Mr Ma told him. "The thing is that this foreign girl has been in Tianjin for a while now, but she doesn't know anyone and she's bored. Don't worry, I'll bring the second young master back here this afternoon. I promise you he'll be as bright-eyed and bushy-tailed as when he left!"

He dragged Ouyang Jue over to the corner of Gongnan Avenue, where they got into a hackney carriage and headed off towards Zizhulin. The brand-new carriages running the route between the old city and the Zizhulin Foreign Concession had big wheels and a fast turn of speed. Underneath, there were fancy foreign-made springs, so you could bounce about without hurting your bottom. The carriage had glass windows on all four sides, so when he was sitting there, Ouyang Jue felt as if he were bathed in light. He could not have told you if it was the brightness that made him feel so happy, or the emotions bubbling up inside his heart.

CHAPTER 4

The Tianjin Foreign Concession at the end of the 19th century

This was only the second time in his life that Ouyang Jue had ever been anywhere near the Foreign Concession.

The first time, he went with his elder brother to buy a kind of waterproof plaster for repairing the roof of their warehouse. This kind of plaster was particularly effective, and it was shipped in from overseas. It was kept in a storehouse on the banks of the White River, right next to the Foreign Concession. In point of fact, he actually didn't set foot inside the concession at all. This time, it was different: he was going right into the belly of the beast.

Flashing past the windows of the carriage were all manner of strange buildings, odd-looking people in bizarre get-ups and peculiar vehicles: in particular, there was a foreigner in a small round hat riding a most unusual vehicle with only two wheels, though he looked perfectly comfortable doing so. Ouyang Jue was quite dumbstruck, and his eyes were practically starting from their sockets; he was so amazed that he completely forgot to talk to Mr Ma. The latter said to him, "You look just like Mademoiselle Xénia when she was walking down Gongnan Avenue the other day."

As he looked into Mr Ma's smiling face, he didn't know what to say.

Suddenly, the carriage stopped, a door opened, and they got out into a different world. On either side of the street were all sorts of buildings: some were topped with spires, while others had square roofs or domes, but they were at least twice as tall as the houses over in the old city. Sandwiched between them as if in a canyon, the unfamiliar atmosphere, silent and dark, made Ouyang Jue deeply uncomfortable. In a daze, he followed behind Mr Ma, who took him through a black wrought-iron gate. Ahead of them lay a cobbled path with flower beds to either side, while the red-tiled roof of a Western-style building could be glimpsed through the trees. Suddenly, the front door was flung open, and someone came running out, laughing with pleasure, fluttering to his side like a huge butterfly. That beautiful flower-like face, that delicious, familiar fragrance – it was Xénia. She looked even more stunning than the first time they had met.

Xénia pointed at him and enunciated clearly, one word at a time, "Ow-my-jaw!"

She laughed, Mr Ma laughed, and once he understood what she was saying, he laughed with them. He now felt as relaxed as he had the previous time they had met; the emotions that he had felt visiting the Temple to the Queen of Heaven and Zhang Xian's pavilion came flooding back. Ouyang Jue had the pleasant sensation of meeting an old friend again.

She happily invited them into her house.

For the first time in his life, he entered a foreigner's residence.

When he looked around him, he was deeply impressed. Every single object he could see was either something he'd never so much as heard of, or something that he had no idea what to do with. There was a sofa, carpets, a chandelier, clocks, curtains, mirrors and oil paintings on the walls, a rocking chair, a fireplace, various pieces of sculpture scattered about, an ornamental cross standing on a pianola... There were various strange cabinets stuffed with myriad ornaments the likes of which he'd never seen before. There were all kinds of foreign books arranged on the shelves of the tall bookcases, and lying on the ground in front of them was a big, curly-haired poodle. Its two huge ears hung softly down on either side of its head. Even though it didn't move, the dog was looking at him, its eyes alert. The dog was amazing too. He had no idea that any of these things even existed – he'd never imagined that such was even possible. What was all of this stuff for? What did you do with it when you had it? He didn't even know how to ask.

The sun shone into the room through the windows shaded by trees, and each and every one of the strange things in that room glittered and shone in the light. The world in which these foreigners lived seemed really strange and magical to him.

Xénia dragged Ouyang Jue off into another room, gesturing at a wooden stand there, holding a pistol and a dress sword in its scabbard. She got Mr Ma to explain to him that they belonged to her father. Her father was an officer in the French Army. When she spoke about her father, she looked very proud, as if she were talking about some kind of hero. She said that this pistol was her father's favourite, and the barrel was exceptionally long. The longer the barrel, the further the bullet would travel. But to shoot this kind of gun for any length of time, you had to raise your other arm to support the barrel. According to Xénia, her father was a famous sniper.

She picked up the dark, shiny pistol and put it in his hand.

It felt very heavy and cold. He had heard that foreign firearms could kill people hundreds of steps away, and he was a little scared. Xénia was looking at his face, and now she smiled and took the gun from his hand. She said something that he didn't understand. Mr Ma translated for him. "Mademoiselle Xénia said she doesn't like these things either."

He wondered how Xénia could know how he felt.

He noticed that there were a number of framed photographs standing on the table. Xénia pointed to them one by one and explained that the bearded man in a military uniform, holding a sabre, was her father. His chin beard was so dark it looked as if it had been painted on with a thick stroke of ink, and his appearance was rather frightening. In another picture, the smiling middle-aged foreign woman was Xénia's mother; although she was dressed in a peculiar fashion, she looked very kind. Mr Ma explained that her mother had stayed behind in France and that Xénia herself would be returning to her after this visit. In addition, there were various pictures of a young girl at different ages. Even at first glance, he could see that they were all of the same person – a charming, kittenish child. Ouyang Jue pointed to Xénia, who was delighted that he had recognised her.

Ouyang Jue had already decided he loved the way she smiled.

Xénia showed him one of the things lying on the mantelpiece: this turned out to be the telescope. She explained that it belonged to her father. Her father liked this kind of monocular because it was very lightweight, and he looked really impressive holding it. All of a sudden, she went over and grabbed it. Then, bubbling over with excitement, she caught hold of Ouyang Jue's arm and went running out of the house with him. She was running in front, while Ouyang Jue and Mr Ma followed behind her, but even Mr Ma had no idea where she was going. The poodle that had been lying on the ground came running out with them too. After loping along behind them for a while, it eventually turned around and went back into the house.

At that time, there were not many houses in this part of the Foreign Concession. Once they had gone two blocks, the buildings were already becoming few and far between, and beyond them was an undeveloped wasteland. There were no fields here; only weeds, clumps of reeds, brambles and bushes. However, once they had gone a few hundred yards, they came across a small white foreign building, standing empty and abandoned. The French Concession was located right by the White River, so behind this house you could see its dark waters and the slick black mudflats. A few wooden boats were moving silently up and down the river, but there was almost nobody on the banks.

This building had never been finished; inside its walls, the weeds and bushes grew waist-high. I do not know why this little house had been built all the way out here in the first place, nor why it had never been completed, but it had now been abandoned for many years. Some rough walls were completely covered with wild vines, which gave this tumbledown building in the middle of nowhere an even greater air of mystery. It was the beginning of summer, so bright yellow wildflowers were blooming gaily everywhere, and it was humming with bees.

Xénia seemed to know this little house well. She took them straight inside and up the stairs. The empty building was surprisingly clean. Probably no one ever came here, since the Foreign Concession was forbidden ground, and it was so far away from the old city. If it had been located there, the whole place would have quickly been reduced to rubble like any other abandoned building, and then used as a latrine. This house, however, was not missing so much as a single brick. Because there were no windows, just gaping holes in the walls, some dry leaves had drifted in, and there were a few scattered bird droppings and feathers.

This little house only had two floors. But there was also a small, hexagonal attic room, hidden within the tower that poked up above the ridge of the roof. When they climbed into the attic up a narrow wooden staircase, the scene changed entirely. There were two narrow window openings looking east and west. Because it was so high up, and the marshlands around were all as flat as a pancake, you could see for miles. Most remarkably, the two windows looked out on two quite different landscapes – one faced the Foreign Concession, while the other looked out towards the old city of Tianjin. Ouyang Jue was interested in the strange world that foreigners inhabited, while Xénia concentrated solely on Tianjin itself. She handed the telescope to Ouyang Jue and asked him to look at the old city, which to her was an incomparably fascinating sight. And indeed, it was a remarkable thing to behold!

Although Ouyang Jue had lived in Tianjin almost his entire life and was familiar with its every aspect, looking from here at the vast old city stretching out towards the horizon, it seemed almost as if a map had been unfurled before him.

Looking from Zizhulin towards the old city, apart from a handful of peasants' huts scattered along the banks of the river, the rest was just a wilderness – clumps of weeds, ponds, and the occasional bit of high ground with a few trees, and here and there the overgrown graves of the poor. To the left was the White River, which encircled this vast area of wasteland like an endless grey ribbon, stretching as far as the eye could see. Just before the White River disappeared over the horizon, there was a small patch of glistening water: that must be where the three rivers joined. He pressed the cool metal of the telescope against his eye and discovered that he could see the two flagpoles in front of the Temple to the Queen of Heaven, but from this distance they looked like two needles. Just to the right of where the glittering waters converged, he could see a small grey box: the Church of Notre-Dame des Victoires. As he looked around, he was surprised to discover so many temples in Tianjin. They were scattered all over the place, in every shape and size, as if someone had tossed a handful of exquisite trinkets across the city – it was really very pretty. Straight ahead of him, surrounded by a moat and low ramparts, and spread out like a huge chessboard with each square crowded with tightly-packed, low-rise buildings, lay the old city of Tianjin. He searched and gradually made out the four gates to the city, and the towers on each of the four corners. However, thanks to the smoke rising from every stove in the city, and the thick mist veiling the moat, even when Xénia showed him how to rotate the upper and lower sections of the telescope in order to focus it, he could not see anything inside the city at all clearly.

Ouyang Jue wanted to explain to Xénia that he lived over there. But they had no language in common, so he had to point to himself, and then in the direction of his home.

She didn't understand and wrinkled her brow. She had a lovely frown, too.

An idea now came to him. First, he pointed to himself and said "Ow-my-jaw", and then he pointed out at the old city far in the distance. Xénia immediately understood – that over there was where he lived. Xénia seemed to admire the ways he found to communicate with her.

How else could they talk to each other?

They introduced to each other the different worlds in which they lived, and in the process they got to know more about one another – but for this they needed the help of Mr Ma.

"It turns out that Mademoiselle Xénia only wants to know about the second young master, and the second young master only wants to know about Mademoiselle Xénia," Mr Ma said with a smile.

As the sun started to set in the west, they had to leave that small house. They both felt a strong sense of satisfaction.

Mr Ma summoned a carriage since he still had to take Ouyang Jue back to the old city. Standing at the door to Xénia's house, when the time came for him to say goodbye and get into the carriage for the journey back, Ouyang Jue felt a curious sense of desolation. He had no idea why he felt this way. He didn't even know whether this feeling came from deep within his heart, or whether he saw the same sadness in Xénia's eyes. Was he really able to read the subtle feelings that she could not help expressing in her blue eyes?

As the carriage started to move, he looked through the glass and saw her standing there – standing stock-still in front of the curlicues and floral sprays of the black wrought-iron gate. As she was left further and further behind, it seemed almost as if she had stepped back inside a painting.

In the carriage, Ouyang Jue had only one thing he wanted to talk to Mr Ma about, and that was Xénia; he never so much as mentioned the paper business. He discovered from Mr Ma that

Xénia was eighteen years old – six years younger than himself. She had arrived in the Foreign Concession on a visit to her father two months ago, but now relations between China and the Western colonial powers had suddenly become much more complicated, with violent resistance against foreign interference, so the situation within the concession had become quite tense. Her father was trying to find some reliable person to escort her home. Mr Ma said, "I know her father well – he's been here for a couple of years now, and he's in charge of the French Concession's garrison and security personnel. Last time, when her father asked me to show her around the old town, it was the first time I'd ever met her. However, I am not on anything like such friendly terms with her as you are. I told her that you are famous around Tianjin for your writings and paintings, and that you have beautiful calligraphy."

"Really?"

"What do you mean, really? I didn't particularly want to tell her about you, but she grilled me about every aspect of your life…"

"Why would she grill you about me?"

"You'll have to ask her that," Mr Ma said with a smile. "I do a lot of business with foreigners, but I have no idea what they are thinking about. She said that you were just like the Chinese man that she'd read about in a novel."

"What novel?"

"I can speak French, but I can't read it. How should I know?"

As they were talking, the carriage passed the Daying Gate. "Why do I feel that the way back is shorter than the journey out?" Ouyang Jue asked.

"It can't be," Mr Ma said, "since we are going the same way."

Mr Ma was as good as his word and escorted the second young master all the way to Gongnan Avenue. By the time they got there, it was already dark. The eldest young master was waiting for his brother in the shop. When Mr Ma came in, he said, "Well, I've brought the second young master back to you safe and sound, but you'd better keep an eye on him. That foreign young lady seems quite fascinated by him."

"I don't know what you expect me to do," the eldest young master said. "How about you stop dragging him off to meet her?"

Everyone was chatting and joking, but they didn't take the situation at all seriously. Then they said goodbye and went their separate ways.

Ouyang Jue did take it seriously, but if you'd asked him to explain what was going on, he wouldn't have been capable. He closed up the shop with his brother, and after giving a few final instructions to the nightwatchman, the pair went home in a rickshaw.

When they got back to the house, they found that Zhang Yi was waiting for them at the door. He said that Old Master Ouyang wanted them to go to his living room as soon as they got back – he was waiting for them there.

On entering the room, they saw that their father was looking very solemn. When they asked why, Old Master Ouyang took out two pictures and laid them down on the table for them to see. When they picked them up, they found that they were looking at two small woodblock colour prints, like New Year pictures. But the subject of the prints was something entirely new to them. One showed a group of people of all ages, some in ordinary clothes, others in army uniforms or dressed as monks, holding sticks that they were using to beat a couple of pigs. Above them, there was a Buddha and a Daoist immortal hanging in mid-air, surrounded by auspicious clouds. This picture was entitled 'Buddhists and Daoists Beat the Foreign Devils'. The other picture was entitled 'Shooting Pigs and Butchering Sheep'. It looked a bit like an illustration of King Yama presiding over the ten courts of hell, but instead of Yama, it showed a senior government official. Some of his underlings were holding up bows and arrows. Opposite them, a black pig was tied to a cross of the kind they have in foreign churches. The black pig had been shot full of arrows, so it was dripping with blood and howling. There was a couplet running down both sides of the picture. On the right, it read, "With thousands of arrows lodged in the pig's body, let's see if these devils dare to make any more complaint." On the left, "As a single knife cuts the sheep's throat, let's see if these animals dare to return."

"When Zhang Yi went out to buy fish this afternoon at the

Flourishing Glory seafood store over on Beidaguan Road," Old Master Ouyang said, "someone was handing these out."

The eldest young master picked up the conversation. "That's a Boxer print. I've seen them before. The pig in the picture represents Jesus – the god that the foreigners pray to in church. This print has probably come here from Shandong Province. The Militia of Righteous Harmony started mobilising there last year, and the government has been struggling to get the situation under control. The fighting has been particularly fierce since the spring."

Ouyang Jue had never seen a picture like this before, and he didn't know much about what his elder brother was talking about, so he kept mum.

"That's what I thought," Old Master Ouyang said. "I've heard that the Militia of Righteous Harmony is fighting under the slogan of supporting the Qing dynasty and killing foreigners, so they aren't attacking the government, just the Westerners. However, there are Westerners living right here in the Foreign Concession in Tianjin, so I am really hoping we are not going to be dragged into this."

"It's true that the market has been a little bit restless recently," the eldest young master replied. "There have been some pretty odd people coming into the city lately, and a lot of rumours, but nothing that you can really put your finger on. Chinese Christians are getting more and more frightened, but I haven't heard of anyone actually being attacked. However, even supposing that they do get butchered, I don't see why we would be targeted since we aren't Christians. As far as I can see, we should come out of this unscathed."

Old Master Ouyang was still worried. He glanced over at the two pictures on the table and said, "Looking at the way things are going, once fighting breaks out, people are going to be killed and there will be arson attacks. Think how many people were butchered in Tianjin thirty years ago when they had all that fighting over the children dying in the Notre-Dame des Victoires orphanage! That was before Jue was even born. We were still living in our old hometown in those days, and it made your hair stand on end just hearing about what went on round here…" At this point, he suddenly turned to his younger son and said, "What have you got to say for yourself?"

Nobody was expecting Ouyang Jue to simply smile and say, "I think those two pictures are completely hideous. The people are as ugly as the devils."

This annoyed Old Master Ouyang, and he spoke sharply to Ouyang Jue. "Has all this learning addled your head? I don't mind if you decide against a career as an official, but you need to keep your ear to the ground – you can't spend all your time thinking about nothing that has happened since the Tang and Song. If the world collapses into chaos, the Confucian classics aren't going to be what saves us." As he spoke, he became angrier, and his voice grew louder. "What happens to our family will depend on the country staying safe and sound, so I want you to put your books aside for the moment. Starting today, I want each of you to keep an eye on our two shops. I need you to be helping your brother."

Ouyang Jue had no idea why his father, quite out of the blue, was taking these stupid things so seriously. However, he didn't want to anger him, so he said quickly, "If that's what you want, of course I will help."

Old Master Ouyang thought for a long time and then said in a measured way, "The most important things to sort out right now are keeping someone on the door and fire prevention. Actually, it is fire prevention that is going to be crucial. Supposing that fighting does indeed break out, we can expect arson attacks. Paper shops are a prime target. I've heard that the Boxers in Shandong and Hebei have been going around setting fire to churches, and they've been burning shops and business premises alongside them. We need to make sure that we have water to hand, and I want you to make contact with the local fire brigade – the brigade here in Tianjin has always been very helpful. If you give them a bit more money, we can be sure they'll put their backs into it if it turns out we actually need them."

The two brothers agreed. "Which of our shops are you going to take?" Old Master Ouyang asked.

"I'll take the Gongnan one," Ouyang Jue said straight away.

No one had a clue why he wanted to be put in charge of the

shop on Gongnan Avenue. Probably he was the only person who understood his thinking. The eldest young master didn't think it important, so he said, "Fine. You've been to the Gongnan shop more often than the other one. The Guyi Street branch is bigger, with more customers, so I'll deal with business there."

With this settled, Old Master Ouyang felt he could relax.

As they emerged from the courtyard occupied by Old Master Ouyang, the eldest young master said to Ouyang Jue, "I don't want you going back to the Foreign Concession again. Otherwise, people will think you're a 'second-class hairy' – one of those Chinese Christians."

Ouyang Jue started, and then said with a smile, "I suppose I might as well go right ahead and join the Boxers." He never paid the slightest attention to current affairs and didn't take his father and brother's concerns seriously.

The eldest young master said solemnly, "I think you had best go back to your rooms and change your clothes. I can smell that woman's perfume from here, and I don't want Shuxian getting upset over it."

Ouyang Jue started a second time. He raised his arm and smelled his sleeves. This time, he could indeed smell her wonderful fragrance quite clearly. Yes, thinking back to the events of that afternoon, he and Xénia had been huddled up together by the tiny attic window the whole time.

CHAPTER 5

Europeans living in China at the end of the 19th century

STARTING THAT VERY DAY, Ouyang Jue was put to work in the Broadlight paper shop on Gongnan Avenue. But his heart was certainly not in it. He was physically present, but his mind was very definitely elsewhere.

Fortunately, the future prosperity of the Broadlight did not depend on him.

This particular branch of the business had been in operation for more than twenty years, and Old Master Ouyang had long ago ensured that it operated on an even keel. Money was paid in and out, carefully registered in the correct ledgers, and his staff knew exactly what they were doing and stuck to the rules and regulations that he had laid down. The eldest young master had then run this paper shop for more than two years, but everything was still done in accordance with his father's wishes. If he wanted to spend a bit more money than usual, he would have to go home and ask his father for it, rather than simply taking it out of the petty cash. This shows just how strictly this Ningbonese family had brought up their sons, keeping them on the straight and narrow. People said that even if the boss didn't set foot inside one of the Broadlight paper shops for three months, everything would still be in apple-pie order. Because of how well run it all was, Ouyang Jue felt very comfortable in the shop, even a little bit at a loose end. He sat there in a reverie, but what he was pondering was not some new painting or work of literature, nor was he worrying about current affairs – he'd never in his life wasted a moment speculating about what was going to happen next. He found that he couldn't stop thinking about that day in the little white building over in the Foreign Concession: the vistas he had seen through the telescope, that pair of sparkling, sapphire-blue eyes, and the charming way in which she'd called him "Ow-my-jaw..."

He didn't find her blue eyes so peculiar any more. They kept shining in his heart, to the point where he sometimes found it difficult to sit still.

For the next few days, he didn't leave the shop at all. It seemed as though he was waiting for someone. But who? Only he knew – he was waiting for Mr Ma.

One day, someone did indeed come to see him, but it was not

Mr Ma. It was Shuxian. She was afraid that he wasn't eating properly, so she'd brought him a packed lunch all the way from the northern part of the city. Shuxian had bound feet, but she couldn't bear to waste money on hiring a rickshaw, so she had walked the whole way. Why on earth hadn't she given the lunchbox to Zhang Yi to deliver? Why did she have to struggle all of this distance by herself? Obviously, she was worried about the second young master; after all, he had never done a day's work in his life before. There were three layers in the finely-woven bamboo lunchbox: one contained stewed pork with radish strips, the next was deep-fried river shrimp, and the last held sixteen dumplings stuffed with pork and cabbage. Each dish was laid out on fresh green lotus leaves. She had cooked and arranged it all herself. Just at that moment, Ouyang Jue felt a little ashamed of himself.

One day, he heard Wei Xiaosan, a clerk in charge of transportation, mention that they had been unable to restock their foreign paper lately. At that time, lithography was more and more popular, since it was fast, produced a really beautiful product and was very cheap. Old-fashioned woodblock printing simply could not compete. The problem was that lithography was a Western technology; the foreigners had the printing presses, and even the paper for it had to be imported from abroad, so they'd always had to go to the Foreign Concession to get the stock they needed. There was a lot of demand for foreign paper – so much that they simply couldn't keep up. When something is selling like hot cakes, you really don't want to find out that you are running out every five minutes. "Well, go and find Mr Ma as quickly as you can," the second young master said, "and when you've found him, bring him here." When he said this, he thought that his opportunity had come. Mr Ma would be sure to come as soon as he was called.

He was not expecting that Wei Xiaosan would shake his head and say, "Mr Ma is a Christian, and the Christians over in the Foreign Concession won't dare come over to the old city – they've heard too much about how the Boxers are coming to kick every 'second-class hairy' out of the place. I've heard that when the Boxers catch them, they cut off their noses and ears and gouge out their eyes."

"How could that possibly be?" Ouyang Jue asked.

"There're much worse rumours going around than that," Wei Xiaosan said. "Everyone is saying that the Boxers are coming here to raze the Zizhulin Concession to the ground."

"How do they think they are going to pull down all of those foreign buildings?"

"I've heard that when the Boxers tie a red rope around a foreign building, it falls over with the first tug."

"I've seen the foreigners' guns. Those things will kill you very dead."

"Everyone says that the Boxers can cast magic spells. Once the hex goes into action, it's as if they are all wearing armour plating – you can't kill them with swords or guns. They can pull out the screws holding the foreigners' machine guns together, so that even those can't be fired, let alone their rifles." Wei Xiaosan spoke with enormous certainty.

The second young master didn't believe a word of it. He said with a smile, "You make them sound even more amazing than the Monkey King. Tell me where I can find these Boxers, since I'd really like to see this with my own eyes."

On this occasion, Wei Xiaosan was left with nothing to say. However, Mr Ma never so much as showed his face.

Two days later, Ouyang Jue left home in the morning on his way to the paper shop on Gongnan Avenue. As soon as he got to the corner, he saw a glassed-in carriage standing there. He could just about make out a figure through the glass, waving to him. When he looked more closely, he realised that it appeared to be Xénia! When he came close, the door suddenly opened, and a white hand stretched out, grabbed his arm, and pulled him so hard he had no choice but to scramble in. As soon as he was inside the carriage, it set off. At that moment, he realised that it was indeed Xénia there with him, and she was alone. This time, Mr Ma had not come. Why was Mr Ma not there? How could she just heave him into the carriage like that? Where was she taking him?

"Where is Mr Ma?" he asked.

Having asked his question, he remembered that they didn't have a language in common.

Xénia seemed to understand his difficulty. She took a note out of her handbag and gave it to him. There were just a few words written on it: "I'm busy today so I can't join you." She pointed to the note and said the word "Ma" in Chinese, to show that the note came from Mr Ma.

He understood and immediately nodded his head, smiling at her.

Xénia was glad that he understood. With a mischievous expression, she pointed to the note and repeated her Chinese word, "Ma… Ma… Ma…"

They both burst out laughing. They had managed to communicate and had the pleasant feeling of having overcome an obstacle.

In the carriage, swaying and bumping along, there was nobody to interpret for them so they would have to rely on themselves. They began with the things in front of them – for example: you, me, carriage, head, lip, eat, look… all of these basic words. They would tell the other one the meaning and pronunciation, and then try and understand what the other meant, and replicate how they said it. Since they were trying to teach each other different words in different languages, it was hard to say who was quick at picking things up and who was slow, who was saying things right and who was mispronouncing them. However, it made them very happy each time they were able to understand the other. But sometimes, whatever they did, they could not make the other grasp what they were trying to say; then they would both just shake their heads with a sense of helplessness. They felt that their different languages functioned as a barrier between them, but it was one that they were determined to climb. In this way, stumbling over each other's tongues, they arrived at Hai Avenue without even noticing it.

Ouyang Jue simply could not understand. Why had she dragged him off? Where were they going? He had no idea how to ask her these questions.

Xénia didn't have the carriage turn into the avenue. After getting out, she didn't take him to her house. Instead, she went straight to the little white building standing all by itself on the edge of the Foreign Concession. Only then did he understand her idea:

she wanted this place to be a secret that belonged to the two of them alone.

They ran in happily. Xénia was in front, her billowing skirt moving playfully through the long-stemmed wild flowers growing amidst the grass. Ouyang Jue had never before enjoyed the company of any woman in this way, and this was a foreign woman, which made him feel an even greater pleasure and excitement. They ran into the building and went straight up the stairs. When they reached the steep, narrow stairs leading to the attic, she turned around and reached out a hand, which very daringly he took. In a shocking gesture, she closed her fingers around his. In the moment that they touched, he could feel just how smooth, delicate, soft and small her hand was. He was entranced.

When they got to the attic, she took out the brass telescope again. This time, she also got out a small rectangular paper box – a cigarette packet but without any cigarettes in it. Inside, it was full of little square cards. She showed him that there were words written on both sides of the cards: on the one side, there were foreign words looking like the squiggles of magic talismans, which he could not understand; while on the other, there were Chinese characters written with a brush. Did the words on both sides of the card mean the same thing? What was all of this for?

Xénia pointed to a tall building in the Foreign Concession with a steeply-pitched roof some way off in the distance. She began by indicating that Ouyang Jue should find it with the telescope, and then she fished out one of the cards from her heap. She was looking at the foreign-language side. Then she handed the card over to Ouyang Jue and got him to read the Chinese on it. As soon as he looked at it, Ouyang Jue made out the word "church".

"Church," he blurted out.

Xénia nodded happily and said "church" in a loud voice in French. Then she took another card from the cigarette packet and handed it to Ouyang Jue. This time, the word on the card was "yes". She was trying to tell him that the tall, pointy building in the distance was indeed the church.

Ouyang Jue read out the word "yes" from the card.

Straightaway, Xénia imitated his pronunciation and said "yes" too. Her enunciation was very clear.

Ouyang Jue nodded and said, "Yes! Yes! Yes! Yes!" He was trying to praise her for getting the pronunciation right.

At that, they both started laughing happily. It felt as if they had made yet another great leap forward in their relationship.

Ouyang Jue said the word "yes" repeatedly, nodding emphatically as he did so. He thought that she was really clever. Who would have thought of using little pieces of card like that – such an excellent way of establishing a bridge between the two of them! Xénia understood that he was pleased with her, and there seemed to be a sense of accomplishment in her smile.

After this, they continued to communicate with each other using these wonderful pieces of card. With the addition of their own native intelligence, they were able to tell each other a lot.

He decided that Mr Ma must have written out the words on the cards for her, so he asked her this. He first wrote out the Chinese word for his surname, and then said, "Ma?" He imagined that she must have heard someone call Mr Ma by his surname.

Sure enough, she understood and immediately found the Chinese character "Ma" in the stack of cards in her hand, and then recited the word that she'd just learned: "Yes." She was really quick on the uptake!

Both of them were enjoying themselves immensely. Neither of them had previously realised that communicating with someone else could be so interesting, and such fun. This French woman was amazingly clever, so charming and loveable.

The gap in the wall where the attic window should be was small and narrow. When they looked out from it, they had to squeeze close together. Yet again, he smelled her bewitching perfume. Now he felt that the fragrance did not come from her clothes, but from her body, from her blonde curls and her smooth, slender neck. Because he was so near to her, he could see the pale down on her neck. He was pressed right up against her soft and warm body. He felt something stronger than excitement coursing through his body, something that could not be expressed in language. His face grew hot, and his heart was hammering.

Just at that moment, she turned her head as if she wanted to say something to him. But in a flash, she saw something blazing in the eyes of the Chinese man standing before her. She didn't need language any more because she understood exactly what he meant.

Her flower-like face was turned up towards his.

At that moment, everything fell silent. Sometimes, true happiness can be a little frightening.

He looked straight into her blue eyes: clear, translucent and pure. Although he had never looked directly into a pair of blue eyes before, he no longer found them strange, and he now saw something in them that touched his soul. There was no need to understand, no need to think. Suddenly, she reached up and kissed him on the cheek.

Maybe it was all too sudden, too unexpected, too quick… too much. Ouyang Jue stood there like a fool, motionless. He didn't know what had happened. If right at that moment everything depended on his instincts, then his instinctive reaction was to freeze; he had no idea what he should do next.

After a long pause, Xénia turned around and searched until she found one particular card in the cigarette packet: "Sorry!"

Ouyang Jue still did not know how to respond. Of course, he ought to say she had nothing to apologise for, but how could he express that? Their ability to communicate with one another seemed to have disappeared.

They were helpless, embarrassed and awkward with one another. The beautiful things that had just been happening between them had been inexplicably brought to a halt.

They walked out of the little white building in silence. At the corner of Hai Avenue, they went their separate ways. Ouyang Jue got into a hackney carriage. After it had gone clip-clopping on its way for a while, Xénia came in pursuit in a second hackney carriage. She handed him a card. When Ouyang Jue looked down at it, the Chinese characters on the uppermost side read, "Tomorrow."

It was difficult to read the expression in her blue eyes. Was it a kind of apology, regret, loss or worry? Or was it a kind of deep desire?

By the time Ouyang Jue had made his way back to Gongnan Avenue, it was past noon.

He ordered a bowl of noodles served with shredded meat at the Gourmets' Belvedere and ate it, but he wasn't paying any attention to what he was shovelling into his mouth. He rose from the table as unsatisfied as when he sat down. He went into the paper shop and greeted the staff absent-mindedly, then plunged into the back room. He thought he wanted to take a nap, but he could only relax his body and not his mind. One of the apprentices brought him a cup of hot tea, and he lifted it to his lips without remembering to take off the lid. This meant that half his cup of hot tea ended up spilling across the table, soaking the account books there. The apprentice told him that they hadn't done any business at all that morning. The last two days, trade had been unusually slow, and there were fewer and fewer customers for any of the shops on Gongnan Avenue. On the other hand, lots of people were going to the temple to burn incense. Wei Xiaosan said that the Viceroy of Zhili Province, Hitara Hala Yulu, had that very morning moved the Front Division of the Wuwei Army to guard the railway in the east of the city. Could that be related to all the strange things going on round here?

Ouyang Jue had no idea.

Wei Xiaosan was not just a good gossip; he was also a good listener. Since he was handicapped by a slight stutter, it was often difficult to make out what he was saying, not least because he always seemed to be full steam ahead. He wanted to tell the second young master all the news he had picked up here and there with as much vim and vigour as possible. However, Ouyang Jue was quite different from the eldest young master; he had never manifested the slightest interest in what was going on in the world, and right now he had even less mind to listen to this rubbish. Instead, he sent him out onto the street to buy two copies of the most recent issues of the *National News*. As a matter of fact, normally he never read any newspaper, but he wanted an excuse to get rid of the man.

As the afternoon wore on, three strangers pushed open the door and came into the shop. They were dressed very strangely. They wore yellow turbans round their heads, and one of them had a straggly full beard, while another was missing part of one ear. The third looked pretty much normal, but the three of them were probably all members of the Militia of Righteous Harmony – the Boxers. They said they wanted to buy some jute paper for printing posters on. They seemed perfectly polite and paid the listed price, which made them greatly preferable to the local hoodlums with their smash-and-grab tactics.

After that, no one came to the shop at all.

Ouyang Jue sat there until closing time, and then he watched the apprentices put up the shutters. When he returned home, having eaten his dinner, he shut himself up in his study. His experiences that day had thrown his mind into confusion, and he now found it difficult to concentrate. However, since he did not want anyone else to notice his state, he decided it was best to stay in his study, where he could be alone. As he could not just sit there idly, and he did not have the presence of mind to read, he thought he might as well practise his calligraphy. He remembered that he had promised a friend to write a scroll for him; however, feeling an absence of inspiration, he had no choice but to write some traditional phrase. He spread the paper out flat and prepared to write the words "Yes, You Must Do What You Can" from the Zuo commentary on the *Spring and Autumn Annals*. When he picked up his brush to write the word "yes", what appeared before his eyes was the word as written by Mr Ma on Xénia's little card… and then he thought back to all the amazing things that had happened during the day. That pair of entrancing blue eyes, the soft down on her neck, her pretty little hands and the kiss she had suddenly given him… all these things sped through his mind. He kept thinking about that kiss – why didn't he feel anything when such a shocking thing had happened to him? He reached out and touched his cheek: no, nothing felt different. He felt again, but still there was nothing: where had the kiss gone? Does a cheek have no memory? He was longing for her to kiss him again like this, so he thought about the card she had shown him with the word "tomorrow" written on it – it was an appointment for the two of them to meet the next day. So, what would happen then?

He could not stop his imagination from running wild, as one incredible scene after another raced through his mind.

The door opened.

Shuxian walked quietly into his study and handed him a small porcelain jar filled with melon seeds that she'd prepared, all white and lovely. She leaned over the high seatback and said in a low voice, "You seemed to be reluctant to talk to your father today."

He was stunned, but after a moment of reflection, he replied, "Yes, business is in a bad way at the moment."

In those days, in that kind of family, business was a matter for men, and women weren't supposed to know anything about it. Shuxian turned the conversation in a different direction. "You seem to have got yourself absolutely soaked in perfume today – I suppose there was another delivery of that scented notepaper. Since Father doesn't like it, I don't think you should keep it in stock."

For a moment, he was stunned again, and having collected his thoughts, he said, "Of course, you are quite right."

"People say that Boxers are pouring into Tianjin from Shandong and Hebei. Xifeng says that they've all come by boat along the Grand Canal, and after all, your brother is working at the shop over on Guyi Street, isn't he? Apparently, the government is sending troops to intercept them, and they are not going to be allowed to disembark."

"I don't know why you pay any attention to all these stupid rumours," Ouyang Jue said as he picked up his pen and started writing.

In the normal way of things, Zhuang Shuxian never said very much. Today, she had broached a couple of different topics because she wanted to know more about what was going on outside. However, since he obviously didn't want to talk, she decided not to disturb him and went back to her own room. That left him to his wild imaginings about tomorrow.

CHAPTER 6

Young Boxers practising martial arts

All that night, he didn't sleep a wink; his head was filled with strange desires and fantasies. The whole time, he kept his back turned to Shuxian, as if he was afraid she might see what was in his mind.

The next morning, he got up early. After breakfast, he set off for the Gongnan store, but when he arrived at that bustling and noisy street he couldn't see Xénia's carriage anywhere. He sat down on an empty stool at a stall by the side of the road and asked for something to eat and a bowl of hot tea, but he didn't eat or drink a thing – he just sat there and waited for Xénia to come. The guy from the stall came over twice and asked him what else he wanted to order; this question was intended to encourage him to eat up and get going. However, Xénia's carriage still had not arrived. He could not wait there any longer, and all of a sudden he remembered that when she showed him the card with the word "tomorrow", she had pointed towards the small white building. Did that mean she would be waiting for him there? If so, she must have been waiting for him for a long time. He immediately hired a carriage to take him straight to Zizhulin.

He was irritated at how slowly the carriage seemed to move.

When the carriage passed Hai Avenue and was still some way from the Zizhulin Concession, he jumped out; an action that the driver found most odd. There was still a long way to go. Why would you walk when you could go by carriage?

He walked because he didn't actually want to go into the Foreign Concession – he would make his way round from the outside. But this section of the road took him through an area of wasteland: full of rocky outcrops, hillocks, grass-fringed ponds and lakes. Although he had a general direction in mind, he began to worry about losing his way as he walked.

However, when he got past a thicket of scrub that had blocked his way and prevented him from seeing where he was going, he found the little white building he was longing to see right in front of him. This time, looking from another angle, he could see the vast and silent White River behind it. Standing all by itself against this empty backdrop, it seemed a little lonely. Was she there waiting for him?

He ran forward as quickly as he could. Twice, he stumbled and fell to the ground because of potholes hidden in the grass. He got up and went on, running faster and faster. There was nothing to stop him. He ran into the yard, but she was not there. He ran up to the second floor, but that was empty too. He was frightened now, and called Xénia's name as if he feared that she had gone forever. When he made his way panting up to the attic, he still didn't see anyone. Just when he was about to turn around and go back downstairs, he was embraced by two arms gripping him tightly from behind. He couldn't see her, but he could see her hands holding tight to his chest. He also smelled her intoxicating perfume – Xénia!

He turned around abruptly, and before he could see her properly, her lovely soft lips were glued to his mouth. Her lips were quivering, and her mouth was so hot! Her delicate nostrils flared as she struggled to breathe, and he found himself gasping for breath too. All of a sudden, his blood was boiling. His body melted into hers as they were engulfed by this hot tide. It seemed like a fairy tale come true: the wild dreams he had indulged in all night were going to happen right here and now.

He was overcome by a desperate madness. This was not just a breaking down of all restraints, an overwhelming release of pressure, an indulgence of every fantasy, rushing in without a thought of what this would mean – he was also excited beyond control by something he had never experienced before: the sight of a naked blonde woman. And this Western woman, was she not also unbearably excited by something she had never experienced before – a foreign lover? In any case, they forgot everything in their urgency to create an extreme pleasure together.

To begin with, he did not dare to look at her; he did not dare to see what was happening between them, so he closed his eyes and let his desires take over. When finally he opened his eyes and saw her expression of pure joy curtained by her golden curls, her naked limbs spread out to reveal her most intimate places, he was himself no more – a brute nature that he had never so much as suspected existed within himself suddenly burst out.

No one would have imagined that such an incredible thing

would happen in a deserted, abandoned little house located between the old town and the Foreign Concession.

Once the storm had passed, they lay there as if dead. Xénia sprawled naked across his body, not moving a muscle. Neither of them moved. Time stood still. Were they enjoying this magical moment?

After an age seemed to have passed, she suddenly called out. They heard a sound below them, and both were startled by it. When they sat up, they realised that someone or something was crouched at the foot of the stairs. At first, Ouyang Jue thought it was a person, but when he had calmed down enough to take a proper look, he realised it was the brown, curly-haired poodle he'd seen a few days earlier at her house. It lay motionless, as if it had been waiting there for a long time, without making a sound. Perhaps it hadn't wanted to disturb them? The dog's eyes looked at them gently, staring fixedly at them until they put their clothes back on and came down the stairs.

Xénia took the cigarette packet full of cards out of her handbag, and looked for one with the word "Papa" written on it to show him. The way she pronounced the foreign word "Papa" in French sounded much the same as the Chinese word. Did that mean Westerners had the same word as us? He felt quite curious.

She pointed to herself and then in the direction of her home. He guessed that her father had sent the big poodle to come and find her and tell her that he was waiting for her at home. She had to go back.

She took him to the corner of Hai Avenue, where he hired a hackney carriage. When the time came for them to part, he realised that her face was filled with an expression of infinite happiness, but also sadness and unwillingness to leave him. He was deeply moved by her emotion. If it were not for the coachman standing there, she would obviously have jumped up to hug and kiss him. When he climbed into the carriage, she ran up to him and showed him the same card as the day before, with a word that was now the embodiment of happiness written on it: "Tomorrow".

From that day onwards, they met almost every day at the abandoned little house standing all by itself on the banks of the White

River – there they would cuddle and kiss each other, snuggling close, before their desires overcame them, and they reached the heights of pleasure together. For them, this house was no longer a deserted building in the middle of a stretch of wasteland, but their paradise, their secret garden. Now, the very different worlds in which they each lived no longer seemed glamorous to the other; all the magic lay within their own bodies. They didn't even need the words on the cards any more. It seemed as though they were naturally able to interpret each other, to communicate in an instinctive way. This natural connection transcended all the obstacles imposed by culture. But would this transcendence be temporary or permanent? But then at this moment, why would they care?

The two of them seemed to be united in their desires. If there was a difference, it was in her – she was more sexually aggressive than him, and that made her quite the opposite of his wife, Shuxian. Xénia was not restrained, passive and submissive the way that Shuxian was, as if she were only doing her duty – her dutiful lack of interest made him feel the same way. Xénia was not like that at all; she was unembarrassed by her desires, and was happy to open herself up to him, taking the initiative in showing him what she wanted, enjoying him and letting him enjoy her to his heart's content. Maybe that was the crux of the matter: she allowed Ouyang Jue to feel a kind of natural satisfaction that he had never experienced before.

Together, they did whatever they wanted, each of them burning with desire for the other. When they caressed each other, they would also talk to themselves, each speaking in their own language, not worrying whether the other could understand or not. Once, she even sang a song very softly, not knowing whether it was sung for him or for herself. He could not understand what the lyrics were about, but he could hear an infinite tenderness and affection in this strange music, of a kind that he had never heard before.

It was a wonderful and magical experience!

Her sapphire-blue eyes no longer seemed at all strange to him. Now they held many more things than the clarity, translucence and purity he had seen before. He could sense their presence because they were also there in his own heart.

Ouyang Jue could not tell anyone about how wonderfully happy he was. On the contrary, he had to make sure that nobody would ever know. He had to constantly change the route by which he travelled to the concession. He had never been there before, but now he discovered what a distance lay between the old city and Zizhulin. Because he had to avoid anywhere where people might congregate, his journey took him ever longer and further away. If he wanted to avoid the banks of the White River, where there were many boats and endless passers-by, it would at least double how far he had to go.

Once, he made a detour that took him into a small village of some thirty or forty families. There were a few semi-submerged, ramshackle old boats by the riverbank, and hung up among the trees to dry there were nets made from fine black fishing-line. The villagers were probably all boatmen or fishermen, but in the open area in the middle of the village someone was practising boxing. Since the spring, a lot of young men were to be seen wandering around without shirts on their backs, practising this kind of rough 'Righteousness Harmony' boxing. As they were going through their moves, they would sing the following song:

> The Heavenly Gate is open wide,
> The Earthly Door is by your side.
> If you want to learn real martial arts,
> Join us! Just set aside your pride.

He didn't know what it all meant, but it was sung to a catchy tune. When he passed through the small village, he was stopped by the villagers who thought he was some 'second-class hairy' Chinese Christian who'd escaped from the Foreign Concession, and he was interrogated for ages before they finally let him go. There was another occasion when he got caught in a downpour. Out in the middle of nowhere, there was no place for him to seek shelter, so he had to work his way under a dense clump of trees. It was more than an hour before the rain stopped, and by that time he was soaked to the skin. When he finally arrived at the small white building, Xénia laughed so hard she ended up out of breath as she stripped him of every stitch of clothing. She liked the way he looked when he was completely naked.

In the Ouyang family, it was Shuxian who was the first to notice that something was up. Although she was very quiet, she was a sensitive and thoughtful person, and there was not much that got past her for all that she might not say anything about it. In that she was quite different from Xifeng; she kept an eye on everything to do with Ouyang Zun, and she talked about it all the time – Xifeng never shut up about anything. Shuxian was alert to the slightest change in Ouyang Jue, but she kept silent, not saying a word on the subject. From the smell of his body, to any number of small changes in his behaviour, to his mood when he came home from work every day, to the things he talked about – she could see that he was very different from the past.

The fragrance that was supposed to come from this foreign scented paper now pervaded Ouyang Jue's hair, his underwear and his armpits. Sometimes his clothes were covered in muck, sometimes they were torn, and then one day he came home in a shiny, brand-new robe. He said that he'd bought it when he went to the Florescent Clothing Company in front of the Temple to the Queen of Heaven, but he had never in his life gone out to buy clothes in a shop before. Normally, every year in the spring and autumn, Old Master Ouyang would have a tailor come from his hometown to make new clothes for the whole family. Old Master Ouyang admired the craftsmanship of Ningbonese tailors and did not care at all for the rough work done by the clumsy, ham-fisted types you found in Tianjin.

She could not understand why he had changed like this.

When she paid more attention to him, she discovered that there were all kinds of things about him that were just not right – for a start, when he was speaking, he would often fail to finish his sentences. When the whole family had dinner together, Father and the eldest young master would be discussing the worsening situation, while he would be absent-minded and could not keep up with their conversation. Ouyang Jue didn't seem to care at all about what was going on; he wasn't worried... none of this seemed to have anything to do with him. Sometimes he would be extraordinarily cheerful, eating much more than usual, and afterwards he would tumble into bed and fall asleep snoring.

One night, Ouyang Jue was the first to get into bed, while Shuxian took off her makeup. When she got into bed herself, she saw that he was sleeping soundly, but he hadn't even taken off his clothes. She was worried that he was working too hard, spending all his time at the shop. She wanted to undress him and put him in a fine silk nightgown, but when she started to undo his collar, she got a nasty shock: what could he have been doing to hurt his shoulder like that? Looking more closely, she realised that it was a bite-mark! Although the tooth marks were not very deep, they had drawn blood – what on earth could he have been up to? As she tugged his robe off him further, it revealed the bright red, clear print of a pair of lips. She stared at it fixedly, for she now understood exactly what was going on.

Of course, there were things that she did not know, starting with the identity of the woman who had left the marks of her teeth and lips on her husband's shoulder and back. In spite of the evidence before her eyes, she still trusted in Ouyang Jue's good character; she simply could not believe that he had been going with a whore. All of his friends were educated gentlemen – all they ever talked about was poetry and painting – where could he have met this woman?

Shuxian didn't get any sleep that night, but she had to listen to Ouyang Jue snoring the whole time.

The following day, Shuxian served him breakfast as usual before he went to the Gongnan paper shop to start work. She didn't show any sign of just how worried she was.

As was his custom now, instead of turning down Gongnan Avenue, Ouyang Jue headed in the direction of the Foreign Concession instead. He was already lapped by waves of lust – he simply did not care about anything else. It wasn't until late in the afternoon that he said goodbye to Xénia and went back to the old city.

After buying a snack to eat on the street, and before going back to the shop to make sure that everything was under control, he decided to turn into the Immortals' Pool Bathhouse behind the

Foundling's Hospital for a quick wash, to clean off the dust he'd rolled in at the small white building.

The Immortals' Pool was the best bathhouse in Tianjin, and it had become very popular over the last couple of years – the wealthiest inhabitants of the city liked to go there to wash and socialise. Inside, there were two pools: one warm and one hot. Having got naked, first you would get into the warm pool to relax for a bit and let your pores open, then you would go for a quick session in the hot tub. The water in the hot tub was very hot, to the point where people would scream on getting in – it would simply scald the filth out of you. After you'd had your time in the hot tub, you'd go back to the warm pool for a scrub, leaving you with an indescribable feeling of freshness and comfort. It was said that bathing here was the nearest you could get in this life to the pleasures of paradise.

Ouyang Jue and the eldest young master made a trip to this bathhouse at least twice a month. It was expensive to treat yourself to a visit to the Immortals' Pool, and most of the people who used it knew each other, at least by sight. Today, Ouyang Jue took off his clothes and glided into the warm-water pool, which was about a metre deep. Everyone was sitting around the sides of the pool, relaxing. Just at that moment, a man scrambled out of the hot tub and walked along the edge of the pool behind him. Then he stopped and suddenly squatted down. Ouyang Jue turned his head and saw that the man's fat, round body had been turned so red by the hot water that he looked like a freshly cooked river crab, still steaming after coming out of the pot. A round face was beaming at him, which he recognised as belonging to Sun Shaojun, who would one day inherit the 'Great Success' soy sauce factory in the city, for all that right now he was a complete playboy. Sun Shaojun leaned over and whispered to him, "So who's the lucky lady that's caught Young Master Ouyang's eye?"

That was an awful shock for Ouyang Jue, who couldn't imagine how anyone could have found out about what was going on. "What on earth are you talking about?" he demanded.

He had no idea what else to say.

Sun Shaojun kept on smiling. "It's not just me that's talking about it. Everyone in the Houjiahou district knows all about it."

The Houjiahou district was located outside the North City, and this was where Tianjin's brothels were situated. When he heard this, Ouyang Jue felt quite relieved – the man was just joking.

"That's the kind of place we'd find you, not me," he said.

But he was not going to get off so lightly. All of a sudden, Sun Shaojun poked at his right shoulder with a fat, round finger and said, "So who put those tooth marks in you? Do tell! I'd love to know which of the girls is quite that energetic!" He started to laugh.

That was most unwelcome news for Ouyang Jue. Could it really be that he had been going around with tooth marks clearly visible on his back? He knew that it must be Xénia who'd bitten him, but he had no idea how to change the subject, so he just sat there feeling awkward. Fortunately, Sun Shaojun wasn't interested in making an issue of it, and he walked away, cracking other jokes.

Ouyang Jue clambered out of the pool and went to the private room he'd hired for the occasion, which came complete with a reclining chair, tea-table, cupboard and standing mirror. He stood naked facing the mirror and then twisted round until he could see his back. Sure enough, there were two rows of tooth marks, which his time in the warm water had made even more obvious.

He didn't feel like going back to the bath again. As he lay on the couch and thought about it, his heart began to hammer. He was quite sure it was Xénia who had bitten him, but when? If it was today, then everything was fine; but if it was a day or two ago, wouldn't Shuxian already have seen it? He thought back to everything they had done over the last couple of days, and he decided that it must have happened the day before yesterday. He could remember shouting out at the time, "Hey! That really hurts!"

He spoke in Chinese, which she couldn't understand at all, but at a moment like that who cares who says what?

If it was indeed the day before yesterday, then when he went to bed last night, Shuxian might well have seen it. The more he thought about it, the more worried he became. She must have noticed something because today when she served him breakfast she'd been different from normal – a little unhappy. Shuxian had always been very polite to him, and normally whenever he went out she would escort him as far as the gateway to the second courtyard where they lived, but this morning she'd stayed behind in their rooms. Ouyang Jue was a sensitive creature, but right now there wasn't a thought in his head unconnected with Xénia, so he hadn't paid any particular attention to his wife's mood. Now, the more he thought about it, the more convinced he was that she knew.

Later, when he went back home, he tried to test her. Shuxian helped him out of his coat and into his slippers as usual, then she heated some water for him to wash his face and made him a cup of tea. At the same time, she instructed Mrs Jiang to go to his study and light a stick of incense there. In every detail, it seemed as though nothing had happened, but his heart was pounding nevertheless. He knew Shuxian only too well; if anything bad happened to her, she would try to cover it up. She would suffer in silence the wounds he had inflicted on her heart.

CHAPTER 7

A gathering of young gentry in the late-Qing

THIS YEAR, the Ouyang family's old scholar tree was very late to flower. Every year at this time, the whole family would be in high spirits, waiting for the blossoms to open and their delicious scent to spread through the house.

When the flowers bloomed just after his marriage to Shuxian, Ouyang Jue had invited a number of his old friends to come round.

That day, he placed a huge painting table out under the big scholar tree and arranged paper, brushes, ink and an inkstone on top of it. The Ouyang family owned a very fine collection of antique scholar's studio paraphernalia. The paper they provided came from Jing County in Huizhou; the ink had been made by Cao Sugong some three hundred years earlier; the brushes were also antiques, made by the master craftsman Zhan Dayou; and the inkstone was carved from Zhaoqing volcanic Duan stone. The dark blue-black Ming-style inkstone preserved the natural unworked stone surface except for the tiny triangular well scooped out at one end – very elegant and refined. It was a really covetable piece! As for the ceramic bowl for washing brushes, the paperweights, the water dropper and the brush holder, they were all just as exquisite. Ouyang Jue's friends had a wonderful time writing poetry and painting the scholar tree flowers over their heads.

On this occasion, Shuxian had made each of her husband's friends a cup of golden-yellow scholar-tree-blossom tea, using dried flowers that the Ouyang family had saved from the year before, in the hope of inspiring them further. Ouyang Jue was so struck by this that he immediately composed a poem:

> *Inspiration has seized my brush,*
> *Pooling ink makes these flowers lush.*
> *There is no need for any bright colours,*
> *Black and white makes a world for lovers.*

This impromptu poem was much admired by his friends, particularly the line "Pooling ink makes these flowers lush", which they thought remarkably successful. At that time, his father – and indeed the whole family – were impressed by how well the whole occasion had gone. Afterwards, Shuxian copied out the poem in her neat and elegant regular script on letter paper, called 'Shades of the Scholar Tree Hall', which the Ouyang family had specially made for them at the Studio of Refined Beauty. Old Master Ouyang said happily that in the future they would hold one of these gatherings for poetry and painting every year when the scholar tree flowered. However, he wanted it to be held in the front courtyard because the main hall for greeting guests was in the courtyard where he lived, which would make the occasion even more impressive. He said that he would be sure to invite some famous writers and artists of an older generation, such as Ma Jiatong, Zhao Yuanli and Meng Xiucun, to join them so they could give a few pointers to these promising young men.

His father's suggestion was very pleasing to Ouyang Jue and Shuxian, and they were really looking forward to it.

Unfortunately, last year it had been one damned thing after another with that wretched old scholar tree, which put the whole idea of a party out of their minds. And now this year the weather was unusually hot, so by the time they got into May it was already roasting. In spite of this, the tightly-packed buds covering the tree refused to open; it seemed as though the flowers were determined to suffocate inside their green wrappings. But if the flowers didn't bloom, wouldn't they just wither away? Were they all going to miss out on the fragrance this year?

But then, no one seemed disposed to care what was happening to the old tree. Old Master Ouyang and the eldest young master spent all day every day worrying about the political situation. Success in business is always intimately tied to current events. No one could be sure if the government was going to crack down on the Boxers to please the foreigners, or whether they were going to join forces with the Boxers to get rid of the colonial powers whose greed seemed to grow with every day that passed. With the political climate so uncertain, nobody was sure what to do, and trade was getting worse and worse. Old Master Ouyang was far too worried to be thinking about holding a party. The second young master also seemed to have forgotten all about it. He hadn't even so much as mentioned inviting his friends round to write a few poems.

It seemed that there was only one person who spared a thought for the old scholar tree, and that was Shuxian. She was prepared to make an effort in the hope of pleasing the whole family. She'd ordered that new brooms be purchased, which would be used to sweep up the flowers, as well as dustpans, bamboo baskets and woven bamboo pans for drying the flowers in the sun. Since people were going to be putting these scholar tree blossoms into their mouths, she wanted all their collection equipment to be new and clean. She was very careful about these things because she wanted to keep the whole family safe; what is more, she wanted Old Master Ouyang to feel that he could relax.

All the manservants and maids in the Ouyang household understood exactly what Zhuang Shuxian was trying to achieve.

However, man proposes and God disposes. At that time, nobody could have imagined what the fates had in store for them.

As Ouyang Jue left the house this morning, he spotted a hackney carriage drawn up in front of the door. Most of the vehicles inside the old city were rickshaws, so where had this hackney carriage come from? In his confusion, he even imagined that Xénia might be sitting inside it – but why would she come to his house? She had never set foot inside the old city after all… Then he heard the carriage door swing open with a bang, and someone jumped out: it was his brother, Ouyang Zun. The eldest young master didn't wait for him to say anything; he just told him to get into the carriage because they were going to Guyi Street. Ouyang Jue knew that Xénia was waiting for him over in the little white house, so he said, "Is it very important? I've got to be over at the Gongnan branch this morning, so how about I visit you this afternoon?"

"Nothing happening at the Gongnan branch could be as important as what I need to talk to you about," the eldest young master said. "I want you to come with me." As he said this, he dragged Ouyang Jue into the carriage. Ouyang Zun was seven years older than his younger brother, and even though the two of them had always got on very well together, he was a much tougher character, as a result of which Ouyang Jue had always been a little afraid of his elder brother. Today, the harsh tone of his voice and the fierce expression on his face meant that it was best to do as he said, even without quite understanding what was going on.

The journey passed in silence as their carriage made its way out of the North Gate. Just as they turned into Beidaguan Road, they realised that something was happening up ahead. There were an awful lot of people milling about, and over by the Zhenwu Belvedere the crowd was packed tight. The atmosphere was very tense, as if something was expected to occur any moment. Just at that instant, someone slapped their hand against the side of the carriage, shouting, "Get out! Get out! Big Brother has just disembarked, and he'll be coming here directly!"

Ouyang Jue pushed the door open a crack and said to the man outside, "We are on our way to Guyi Street... we've got our business over there."

As soon as he said this, the man's voice rose in curses. "I don't care if you're the motherfucking magistrate, I want you to piss off out of there. Haven't you heard? When Big Brother arrives, officials get off their horses, and army officers get out of their carriages to pay him their respects!" With that, he gave the door to the carriage a violent tug which almost pulled Ouyang Jue out with it.

Ouyang Zun realised that the situation could easily turn nasty, and he said hurriedly, "Of course, of course, whatever you say. We'll get out right this minute."

The two brothers made haste to get out of the carriage, paid the driver, and walked in the direction of Guyi Street as quickly as they could. Neither of them dared to so much as look at the person who had shouted at them to get out.

That day, there were probably three times as many people on Guyi Street as normal; you might have imagined that there was a temple festival going on. Looking more closely, it quickly became apparent that the pedestrians walking up and down were not the usual shoppers – almost all of them were men; there seemed to be very few women out and about. Most of the men were big, tanned and strong; they looked like farmers. However, they weren't carrying anything other than maybe a backpack. Some of these men were armed with huge broadswords, with red tassels hanging from the hilt; others were carrying spears; and there were even some people just with hoes or elm-wood clubs. An enormously tall, bald-headed man emerged from the crowd opposite them. He suddenly stopped and glared at them, and then he asked them a question in a tone as resounding as the striking of a bronze gong. Ouyang Jue didn't hear what he said and asked him to repeat it. This annoyed the huge man, and he shouted, "Are you a starer?"

His tone was terrifying. He was asking them whether they were Christians or not: that is, second-class hairys. At that time, Christians in church were thought to fix their eyes upwards, looking towards God. As a result, non-believers cursed them as 'starers' or 'second-class hairys'. Foreigners were called 'Western hairys', and that made Chinese converts 'second-class hairys'. However, 'starers' was more common in Shandong as a term of abuse for Chinese Christians; people in Tianjin normally just called them 'second-class hairys'. Ouyang Jue had no idea what he meant, but his brother was quick to react. With a smile, he said, "I don't know how anyone could fall for that kind of mumbo jumbo. We work at the paper shop up ahead. If you need any paper, be sure to come and find us."

The bald man looked them up and down and then walked away without another word. It was as terrifying as brushing shoulders with a tiger.

The eldest young master dragged Ouyang Jue down a small side-street running past the Azure Clouds Inn. The alleyways leading off Guyi Street on both sides of the road got narrower the further you went, until the walls were pressing right up against you, and you had to turn sideways and breathe in to let someone coming the other way get by. He led Ouyang Jue down one of these narrow lanes and then turned into a tiny courtyard. There was a cramped little room leading off from the courtyard, in which someone was sitting. When he saw them, he stood up. The man was wearing smoked glasses and had a small moustache; Ouyang Jue had never come across him before.

After sitting back down again, the man took off his glasses and sat there squinting at them. There was something about him that seemed familiar. He said, "Second young master, it's me, Mr Ma."

It was only then that Ouyang Jue recognised him: Mr Ma from the Foreign Concession. Since when had he grown a moustache? Before he could ask, Mr Ma said, "It's part of my disguise."

"Why on earth would you need to go about in disguise?" Ouyang Jue asked.

By this time, the eldest young master had worked himself into a rage. He now cut in and said to Mr Ma, "Tell him everything!"

After hesitating for a moment, Mr Ma said to Ouyang Jue, "Second Young Master, you've got to stop going to that tumbledown old building over in the Foreign Concession. If you go back again, they'll kill you!"

He spoke quickly, as if something was terribly wrong.

"How do you know?" Ouyang Jue asked curiously.

"I am not the only one – there are plenty of people in the Foreign Concession who know all about you, not to mention the Chinese folk who do business over there. They have seen you going to the house every single day, and they've seen Mademoiselle Xénia go to join you. You mustn't blame me. In the normal way of things, I wouldn't say a word, not a word – especially not to your elder brother. But with the way things are going, I'm afraid you are going to get yourself killed."

"So who else knows about us? Does Mademoiselle Xénia's father know?" Ouyang Jue asked.

"It is because I am scared that her father does know that I've come to find you. Her father is a nasty piece of work – if he finds out about this, he'll shoot you down like a dog, and I daren't think what he'd do to Mademoiselle Xénia. You mustn't see her again. He's got a couple of hundred soldiers under his command, and he could set them to go after you. These people aren't just armed with rifles, they've got machine guns! They are the best-armed troops in the French Concession!"

Ouyang Jue wanted to ask more questions, but all of a sudden the eldest young master raised his hand and with a *bam* slapped his brother full across the face. He hit him so hard that Ouyang Jue fell off his chair, with one shoe flying off his foot.

Mr Ma gave a horrified screech.

Ouyang Jue was stunned at the sudden blow. Since they were children, his brother had never hit him, let alone struck him with such force. It showed just how angry he must be.

His head was spinning with the blow, and his ears were ringing.

Mr Ma rushed over to help him to his feet. He could see the veins standing out on the eldest young master's forehead, his eyes staring horribly. He was shaking violently as he stood there in silence. It seemed as though he might yet explode with rage again.

Mr Ma was appalled and didn't know how to ameliorate the situation. He just said, "This is all my fault, blame me... I shouldn't have said anything... I shouldn't have come!" But he was still determined to try to convince Ouyang Jue of just how serious the situation was. "I have to tell you... Second Young Master, under no circumstances whatsoever should you go back to the Foreign Concession. Ever since yesterday, there have been a lot of foreign warships at anchor on the White River – they've come from all over the place, and Zizhulin is filling up with foreign soldiers. They've set up the Allied Army Headquarters at the Gordon Hall over in the British Concession. The fighting is going to start pretty soon, and when it does they'll attack the old city. Right now, if you get stopped by one of those foreign soldiers, they're going to kill you first and ask questions later. Besides which, Boxers have been pouring into Tianjin from Shandong and Hebei – if they think you're in secret communications with the Westerners, they'll kill you too. Mademoiselle Xénia is French, after all!"

The eldest young master suddenly found the words to express his anger; even though he didn't say much, he spat out each question with concentrated venom. "What kind of a bastard are you? How could you do this to us? Do you know how upset Shuxian and Father would be if they knew? Are you trying to kill them? People in the Foreign Concession know all about it, so are you telling me nobody in the old city has heard too? Are you trying to ruin our family? What on earth are we going to do?"

When he said this, he seemed overwhelmed with anger – almost apoplectic with rage. Ouyang Jue was so appalled that he fell to his knees in front of him. But his only reaction was to scream, "Go and get yourself killed – I don't care any more! As far as I'm concerned, I don't have a brother!"

He turned round and flung the door open. Marching out, he slammed it shut and stalked off.

There were now only two people left in the room: Ouyang Jue and Mr Ma.

Ouyang Jue was speechless for a long time, but Mr Ma said to him, "If you want to blame someone, blame me and not your elder brother. He's worried about you – you're in a very dangerous situation! You must know that the fighting is going to start pretty soon. The Westerners, the government and the Boxers are all spoiling for a fight. The foreigners over in the concession are moving in more troops every day, and now they're bringing up these huge guns. As of today, nobody is going to be allowed to enter the Foreign Concession, and it is not going to be easy to get in or out of the old city either. As a Christian, I wouldn't dare set foot over there now. I risked my life to come here even in disguise, all because I wanted to make sure you understand the risks you are running. Listen to me, I am begging you, don't go there again!"

There was only one thing Ouyang Jue wanted to know. "Have you seen Mademoiselle Xénia?"

This question shocked Mr Ma. He realised that the second young master wasn't grateful to him at all; he only cared about her. He shook his head and said, "No. I saw her about ten days ago when she asked me to buy her a harmonica of the kind that foreigners like to play. I haven't seen her since."

Ouyang Jue immediately thought back to how charming Xénia had looked when she sang that song to him up in the attic room. He decided that she must want the harmonica so she could play it for him.

"Could you take her a message from me?" he asked Mr Ma. "Just a message... that's all I want you to do."

Mr Ma now decided that the second young master must have been bewitched. He might seem clever enough, but that just served to cover up an underlying inability to grasp the facts of life. However, since it was useless to try to talk him out of it, Mr Ma wasn't going to waste his breath. He just said, "Fine."

"Tell her to meet me at that little white building this afternoon. Tell her to wait for me, and I'll be there as soon as I can." Ouyang Jue paused for a moment and said impulsively, "No matter what, I have to see her again. I have to see her even if they kill me for it."

He was determined to go.

Mr Ma could never have imagined when he took the second young master to Xénia's house that within a couple of weeks they would be engaged in such a passionate affair that he would be risking his life to see her. The only conclusion he could reach was that the second young master had gone insane. He didn't say another word, though, because it would have made no difference. If the man wanted to get himself killed, that was his choice; he'd done his best to prevent it. He put his smoked glasses back on and hurriedly said goodbye.

Once Mr Ma had gone, Ouyang Jue felt uneasy. He believed that he had wasted the whole morning on all of this palaver without being able to make his way out to where Xénia was sure to be waiting for him. She would have been there all this time, and he wasn't able to be with her. Xénia would have been worried about him, but she would have stayed at her post – waiting for him. What should he do? He couldn't just leave her there. He could see her solitary figure standing sadly in front of the little white house, as lonely in the midst of that wilderness as the house itself. Right at that moment, he wanted to be by her side.

CHAPTER 8

A Boxer in charge of supplying munitions

SOMETIMES THE POLITICAL situation changes like the weather, in the blink of an eye. Yesterday and today can be quite different.

Over the last few days, Ouyang Jue had thought only of Xénia – nothing else had any meaning for him, and he simply ignored it. However, today he finally realised that what was going on in the rest of the world would have an impact on their relationship, and that made him pay attention. Now he discovered that things were really happening, and that disaster was upon them all.

He emerged onto Guyi Street and ran in the direction of the Beidaguan Road to hire a rickshaw. That took him as far as the southeastern corner of the city, but when they got past the rice milling works, the trouble started.

At that time, the rickshaws plying up and down the roads were all imported from Japan: they were known as 'Dongyang' rickshaws. At some point, it became standard that each of these Dongyang rickshaws would have a piece of paper stuck on the back, with the words 'Taiping Rickshaws' written on it. If you didn't have that piece of paper, you weren't allowed to work. It wasn't necessarily the Boxers who would stop you; there were plenty of local gangsters who were happy to cause trouble for rickshaw-pullers, not to mention taking advantage of this opportunity to extort money from them. The rickshaw that Ouyang Jue was riding didn't have one of these 'Taiping' labels, so it got stopped again and again, and he was only allowed to pass after handing over some silver.

The further he went, the more troublesome it became; sitting in a rickshaw made him a target, so he decided to get out and walk. As he walked along, he saw a group of people run past, screaming and shouting, in the direction of the Buddhist nunnery in the northeastern part of the city. They said they were going to watch the Boxers burn the church there. Others yelled that they were going to Dragon's Head Point because people were ripping up the railroad tracks out there. All of a sudden, Tianjin was filled with shouting, as its people sustained one shock after another. He didn't know if there was a word of truth in any of it.

When he arrived at the Daying Gate, he realised that the carriages that normally went back and forth between the old city and Zizhulin were nowhere to be seen. The government had even ordered soldiers to set up roadblocks to check on passers-by, and they were backed up by Wuwei troops. Their uniforms bore the character 'Ma' front and back, so they must have been members of the Left Division of the Wuwei Army, under the command of the governor of Zhili Province, Ma Yukun. There were also some people with red or yellow turbans on their heads – members of the Militia of Righteous Harmony, otherwise known as the Boxers. They were asking all kinds of questions of the people who came and went, and they seemed to be really strict about it, but it wasn't clear if they were part of the same thing as the soldiers.

Ouyang Jue felt as though the whole world were against him: clearly, he was not going to be able to get into the Foreign Concession this way. However, if he wanted to make a detour round the southern end of the old city, which was very sparsely populated, he would have to take a very circuitous route. He'd never been that way before, and he had no idea how long it would take. He wolfed down a meal at a roadside stall and bought a couple of buns stuffed with bean paste to take with him; then he headed out west. There were fewer and fewer people to be seen on the roads. It was only when he went past the Temple of Buddha's Light outside the walls that he encountered a crowd. In order to avoid attracting attention, he left the main road and headed out across country. When he crossed the fortified encampment that was built during the Second Opium War by the Qing General Sengge Rinchen, he found it full of sodden, swampy potholes. He had heard that this place was called 'Bluefield', but he'd never been here before – nevertheless he was quite sure he was going in the right direction to get to the Foreign Concession. He pressed on, and gradually vanished from sight as he went deeper and deeper into this wasteland with its stands of straggly trees, scrubby vegetation, stagnant ponds and marshes.

The southern part of the city had never been built up: it remained a wilderness with lakes scattered here and there. This was a waterlogged swamp, barren and uninhabited. It was very difficult to negotiate all of the obstacles this terrain placed in your way; as you turned this way and that, it was easy to become disoriented. Ouyang Jue was a scholar who'd spent his entire life in his study; how could he possibly make his way across this wasteland? Having managed to skirt first the edge of a large marshy mere and then a lake, he forced a path through a dense stand of tall reeds, only to emerge at the edge of an area of greensward.

He thought of lying down on the grass for a while to rest his aching feet, but when he stepped forward he realised it was nothing but a thick patch of duckweed. Under the duckweed was a dark and frighteningly deep pool. He tumbled in, unable to stop himself, as the ground suddenly disappeared beneath his feet and the icy waters engulfed him up to his chest! He thought that at any moment now the black waters would close over his head – he didn't know how to swim... he was going to die! He screamed "Help!" but in this vast wilderness there was nobody to hear him call. It was at that moment that his feet touched the bottom. He wasn't going to die after all! Struggling with all his might, he finally managed to wrench himself out of the waterhole that had so nearly been the death of him.

Once he had made his way out of the dangerous reed beds fringing the edge of the marsh, he found that up ahead there were a handful of scattered small villages. Ouyang Jue didn't dare go anywhere near these houses because he didn't want to get into trouble again. He gave them a wide berth. As the sun slanted towards the west, he finally saw the spires of the Foreign Concession rise up ahead of him. Now he was filled with hope, and he pressed forward. He could see not just the houses big and small but also the dirt roads running between them, glittering in the setting sun like golden belts laid out across the dark land, shrouded by the shadows of coming night. He thought of how long Xénia must have been waiting for him in that small white house, so he quickened his pace. But all of a sudden, he caught sight of a couple of people standing on the road. His eyesight was sharp; he could see that it was a group of foreign soldiers with guns on their backs. He remembered what Mr Ma had told him that morning: as of today, the Foreign Concession would be in a state of siege.

To his mind, the building he was heading for ought to be somewhere on the other side of the road, but to get there he would have to cross the dirt road up ahead. Since it was now guarded by foreign soldiers, he'd have to wait until it got dark and then make a run for it. There were too many waterfowl in the reed beds all around; if you tried to sneak past that way, they would immediately give the alarm, and then the soldiers would discover his location.

He noticed a patch of forest not far away to his right, so he decided to go and hide there, to rest his legs and recover some of his strength. He walked cautiously over towards the woods and found a copse within it where he could stay concealed. He began by removing the sopping wet robe that was clinging to his body and hung it up to dry in the trees. Then he found a puddle of rainwater and washed the mud off his face. He now realised that the slap his elder brother had dealt him that morning had left his face badly swollen, and when the water touched it there was a stinging pain; the skin must be broken somewhere. He wolfed down the bean-paste-filled buns he'd brought with him and crouched down by the side of the pond to gulp some water, without giving a thought to whether it was dirty or not.

He was about to sit down and take a rest, leaning against a tree, when suddenly a couple of men leapt out from hiding in the bushes by his side. Before he could even see who they were, a wad of cloth had been forced into his mouth, and then a heavy jute bag was pushed down over his head. Immediately, everything went pitch-black. These men were very strong; in a flash, they had him down on the ground, turning him over and over as they bound his hands and feet. Ouyang Jue thought his time was up. He'd fallen into the hands of the foreigners, and they were going to kill him.

Once he had been hogtied, gagged and blindfolded, Ouyang Jue was picked up and carried for a certain distance, and then put down again. When he was put down, the man almost threw him to the ground, but by that time he was already beyond feeling any pain. He thought they must have taken him to the Foreign Concession, but then after a while he was lifted up again and carried a further distance, this time by two people – one carrying his feet and the other his head. Probably the man who'd carried him to begin with was tired, so it was now the turn of the others. After going some distance like that, he was handed over to be carried by one man again. His head was covered so he couldn't see a thing, but he did hear them walking across grass and then wading through water, so it sounded like they were still moving through the marsh. Where were they taking him? The Foreign Concession wasn't that far away... Maybe these weren't foreign soldiers after all! Whoever they were, they were strangely silent; in fact, they didn't say a word from start to finish.

After what seemed like a very long journey, finally they stopped; it appeared that they had reached an area of flat land. Again, Ouyang Jue found himself thrown to the ground. This time he landed hard on his left knee, and it was extremely painful. However, he was expecting to be killed at any moment, so this injury didn't really impinge much. With one ear pressed against the ground, he could hear the sound of horses' hooves getting closer and closer, and the odd muffled voice. Then he was picked up again and flung across the back of a horse. His body was arranged so his stomach lay against the horse's back, his head hanging down on one side of the animal's flanks and his legs down the other side. He was now aware that these people were speaking Chinese. If they weren't foreigners, who could they possibly be? His head was still covered, so he couldn't make out what they were talking about.

Then the horse started galloping, and his kidnappers rode off alongside him.

His ears were ringing with the sound of galloping hooves, and his body jerked up and down on the horse's back. He felt dizzy, as if his head was about to split – any moment now his brains would come bursting out. His stomach was churning, and his spine was about to snap in two. He wanted to call out "I don't want to live! Kill me now!" but there was a gag in his mouth, so he couldn't say a word. He was having more and more difficulty breathing, and then he slipped out of consciousness.

PART II

CHAPTER 9

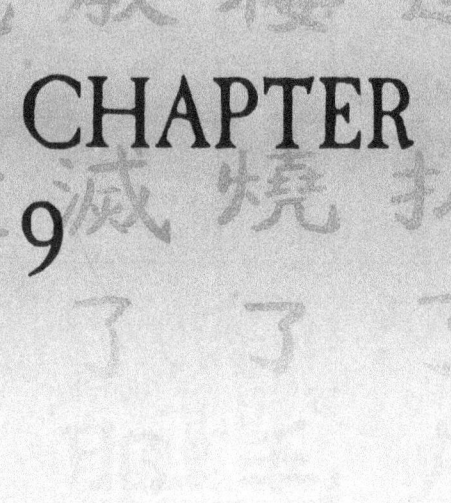

Boxers pouring into Tianjin from Shandong and Hebei Provinces

When Ouyang Jue came to his senses, he couldn't see a thing. He thought he must have gone blind because he could hear perfectly well; he could hear people talking, the whinnying of horses and the sound of something going *pok… pok…* at regular intervals. He had no idea what that was. But there was no light at all. Had he perhaps died and gone to hell? He shifted and immediately felt a pain in his shoulders where they had been bound, and a sharp stabbing agony in one knee. The pain in his knee was probably caused when he'd been thrown to the ground. At that moment, he remembered everything. The ropes that had been used to bind him had gone, and the sack that had covered his head had been removed, so why was everything still pitch-black? He blinked, and he could feel that his eyes could still move in his head; he worked his jaws, and he could hear the click of his teeth closing together quite distinctly; he pinched his arm, and he could feel that too – obviously he was still alive. So he patted the ground around his body and discovered that he was sitting on the floor of a building with his back leaning against a rough wattle-and-daub wall. There seemed to be a lot of dried straw scattered across the floor, which was probably some kind of hay.

Now he knew that he was locked in a room, and it was very dark, which meant it was probably already the middle of the night. As to who had taken him prisoner, he had no idea; he couldn't even begin to imagine.

Not long after this, there was a sudden loud bang, and he was bathed in a dazzling white light, too strong for him to be able to open his eyes against it. He could make out a black figure caught in the light, and the dark shape of a strongly-built man came walking towards him. A shadow fell across him. Then the dark figure shouted at him, "Are you a spy for the foreign hairys?"

Now Ouyang Jue could be quite sure that he had not fallen into the hands of the French. However, he was still locked up in a dark room. How long had he already been imprisoned there? How many hours had passed before he woke up? He simply could not tell. Then the door opened again, and once more he was dazzled by the bright light. It wasn't the middle of the night after all, but broad daylight. The reason it was so dark inside the room was that all the doors and windows were covered in heavy cloth.

This time, a group of men came in, two of them holding torches. Once they were inside, they slammed the door shut. He didn't understand why they didn't just leave the door open – it was daytime after all. Why go through all this rigmarole of closing the door and lighting torches? The flickering flames illuminated the terrifying scene before his eyes. The powerful-looking man who'd entered first was now sitting on a bench in the middle of the room. His hard body looked as strong as iron, and the flames touched parts of his deeply tanned face with light while the rest was submerged in the darkness. The other men were lined up behind him on both sides of the room, each one more grim-faced than the last. This was a very impressive spectacle, and he found himself overawed – he felt almost as if he were standing in a temple to the God of War. Looking at these men again, he realised that they were dressed very strangely. They had blue turbans on their heads, blue sashes around their waists and blue puttees wrapped around their legs; broadswords were hanging by their sides. When he looked at their get-up, he knew they had to be from the Militia of Righteous Harmony. He could never have imagined that the Boxers would already be in a position to put on such a show of strength in Tianjin.

The large man sitting opposite him barked out the same question as he had asked before: "Are you a spy for the foreign hairys?"

"My family runs a paper shop," Ouyang Jue explained, "and we're not Christians. In fact, none of us speaks a word of any foreign language. How could I possibly be a spy?"

He was telling the truth, and because it was true, he spoke very naturally.

"What were you doing over by the Foreign Concession?"

He didn't dare mention Xénia, so he had to make something up. "We'd run out of foreign paper for the shop. We always get our foreign papers from the concession. I went to collect fresh stock, but I wasn't allowed in. In order to get home, I was forced to take various backstreets." This was all invention, but the stuff about foreign paper was perfectly true, so he was able to answer smoothly.

"Why is the right side of your face all swollen?"

Ouyang Jue was a poor liar. But this was a matter of life and death, so the lies were forced out of him. Maybe the next lie would be the one that saved his life! "One of those foreign devils hit me," he said. "He just came forward and slapped me right across the face." It might be a lie, but it sounded perfectly reasonable.

After hearing him out, the big man was lost in thought for a moment. Then he turned his head and said, "Can someone ask Third Brother to come over – this is one for him!"

The door was opened again, and a man entered through a dazzling shaft of light. His skin was very pale, and his complexion was fresh and clear; he had elegantly arched eyebrows over long-lashed eyes, and he entered with a swagger. On entering, he greeted the big man as "Elder Brother". This Elder Brother handed Ouyang Jue over to Third Brother and left, taking his entourage with him.

That meant that only Third Brother and a man with a torch were left behind in the room. Third Brother didn't seem at all threatening; he spoke very straightforwardly, without wasting his breath. "I'll get someone to bring you something to eat," he said. "I'm not going to keep you tied up, but you need to understand that you are not allowed out of this room – you two are going to behave yourselves. If you need to take a shit, then do it over there. If one or the other of you so much as sticks your nose outdoors, there'll be someone there to cut your head off." As he spoke this final sentence, his tones were arctic.

Why did Third Brother keep talking about "you two", "one or the other of you"? By the glittering light of the torch, Ouyang Jue realised that there was another person sitting against the wall in the opposite corner of the room. The man seemed to be very small and thin – almost skeletal. Because that part of the room was dark, not illuminated by the light from the torch, Ouyang Jue couldn't make out what the thin man looked like.

At the same time, Ouyang Jue noticed several thick elm poles lying across the floor – apparently, this building had been used as a stable before being converted into a makeshift prison. Not long afterwards, someone brought in a tureen full of congee, a couple of cornbread buns and two bowls. Third Elder didn't say another word, but instead swept out with his men. Once the door fell to with a bang, it was locked from outside. Immediately, the whole room was enveloped in stygian darkness; not the slightest glimmer of light made its way in, and it was impossible to see what was going on outside. It seemed really odd: why were they so determined to keep them locked up so tight? Was it just because they didn't want them to know what was going on out there?

As soon as he smelled the congee, Ouyang Jue was overwhelmed with hunger. He felt his way over to the food, grabbed hold of it and ate it, wolfing down great mouthfuls. The thin man also groped his way over from the opposite side of the room, and the two men gobbled down everything on offer as greedily as if they had been offered a feast for the gods. In a trice, the dishes were cleared. However, not long after the last mouthful had been swallowed, Ouyang Jue's stomach began to ache. Soon it was unbearable. He felt as if he'd been swallowing hard, sharp-edged stones. He pressed his hands against his stomach and rolled around on the ground – he felt as if his stomach was going to burst.

"How many days has it been since you last ate?" The thin man's question reached him through the darkness.

Ouyang Jue couldn't see the man, but he could hear something odd in his voice, which seemed unusually hoarse.

"I have no idea how many days I've been imprisoned. Do you know?" Ouyang Jue asked.

"When I was brought in, you were already lying over there unconscious. I've been here for two days, so you must have been here longer," the thin man said. "That means you haven't had a thing to eat for days and days, and now all of a sudden you've wolfed down a whole lot – no wonder your stomach can't cope."

Having said these words, the thin man clambered over to the door and brought him a bowl of water to drink, which he'd got from somewhere or other. He also helped him to bend his legs, so he could lie curled up in a ball as he tried to endure the pain.

When his agony was at its worst, for some reason he kept calling

Shuxian's name. Of course, the thin man didn't know who he was shouting for.

As the pain began to abate, he gradually drifted off to sleep. He did not know how much time had passed before he woke up again into the same blackness. The thin man was sitting by his side, and he told him that a whole day had passed. Twice during the course of that day, someone had come in to bring them food, but the thin man had not tried to wake him up because he thought it would be more important for him to sleep than eat. "My family owns a medicine shop," the thin man said, "and I know a bit about doctoring. Right now, you shouldn't be eating anything – just drink more water, and get that food out of your system. Once you start feeling hungry again, you'll be pretty much back to normal."

The thin man brought him a bowl of water to drink and then remarked, "When Elder Brother was questioning you yesterday, I could tell that you aren't a spy – I am not a spy either. Who could I be spying for? Last year, a friend of mine took me to church, and I ended up going a couple of times, that's all. I never even worked out what denomination those people belonged to. Are you a Christian yourself?"

"No. I don't know anything about that sort of thing…" Ouyang Jue said feebly. Then he asked, "Did they arrest you because they thought you were a Christian?"

"Oh, no. One of the families over in the next village owes my family a lot of money, and they've been trying to weasel out of having to pay it back. Those people really hate us. When the Boxers turned up, they denounced me as a spy in the pay of the foreigners, giving information to the priest at the church. They want me dead so that they won't have to repay any of the money they owe us. The moment the Boxers heard that I was a spy, they arrested me and brought me here."

"What will the Boxers do to you?"

"They'll cut my head off. Don't you even know that? As far as the Militia of Righteous Harmony is concerned, being in league with the foreigners is the worst crime you can commit – of course they are going to cut my head off!"

"Tell them the truth."

"They don't know anything about me, so why would they believe a word I say?"

"So what are you going to do?"

"There's nothing I can do. I've been beaten up a couple of times, but now they don't bother with that any more. They said that they would send someone to our village to ask around, and if anyone is willing to guarantee me, they'll let me go. If no one is willing to speak up for me, they'll cut my head off. Now it's just a matter of waiting and seeing if anyone in our village is willing to vouch for my character. This group has really strict rules – they don't go around killing people just for the hell of it. But if there is no one ready to guarantee me, then they'll think I really am a spy, and in that case they'll kill me."

"If you're not a spy, someone is sure to come forward…"

"I'm not so sure. After all, I am a Christian. With things as they are, who would dare to speak up for a 'second-class hairy'? I'm pretty sure I'm going to die. Do you know how many 'spies' these people have killed? Once their heads have been cut off, the bodies are all thrown into a pit behind the village."

Ouyang Jue sighed and said, "Is it likely that they will send someone as far as the old city of Tianjin to find a person who can guarantee me? But if no one goes to get evidence… if no one comes forward to speak on my behalf, then I'm going to die too."

He felt as if his future was just as dark as the room in which he was imprisoned.

When death appears imminent, it is only through speech that you can find a temporary relief from fear and hopelessness.

Confronted with the prospect of his demise, Ouyang Jue was no longer aware of the pain in his stomach. For him, the most important thing was to work out what was going on with the Boxers. He had never paid the blindest bit of attention to current affairs and knew virtually nothing about the Militia of Righteous Harmony, but he wasn't going to be hurried to a premature death without making an effort to find out what they were up to. He had no intention of just sitting there helplessly waiting for them to come and kill him. Above all, he wanted to run away. He was still determined to find Xénia. He had no idea what kind of state she would be in.

She must have been waiting for days and days – she would be so worried and anxious. When he imagined how panicked she must feel, an almost overwhelming urge to escape came over him. "Can't we run away?" he asked the thin man. "Do you know this place at all?"

"Dream on! Even if you grew a pair of wings, you wouldn't be able to get out of here!" said the thin man in a hoarse voice. "We're being held in the Gao Family Village by the Xiaonan River. This group of Boxers is under the direct leadership of Liu Nineteen, the head of the Qian Division. It would be easier to get out of the imperial prison in the heart of the Forbidden City than to get out of here."

"The imperial prison? Do you mean there are other important people held here?"

"You don't understand. The reason this place is so strictly guarded is not that they're keeping anyone prisoner – they're protecting Liu Nineteen himself. Right now, it's not just the foreigners who want him dead; there are plenty of rich and powerful Christians living over in the southern parts of Tianjin who'd be happy to slip a knife between his ribs! You must have heard about what happened to Shi Shiyuan over at Yangliuqing."

"I never heard a word," Ouyang Jue said.

"Have you been living under a rock? Shi Shiyuan was a really important guy over in Yangliuqing Township. He had his own men, and he'd got them armed to the teeth with guns. He was a Christian convert – of course, he didn't really believe, but he wanted to take advantage of the foreigners' prestige to kick other people around. After the Boxers arrived, he set up a fake Militia right there in his township."

"What do you mean by fake Militia?"

"Well, it wasn't real, was it? The Boxers only attack foreigners and Christians. Since when would a Christian be allowed to join the Militia of Righteous Harmony? In a flash, he had thirteen groups set up, with himself as the leader. He actually had the gall to send a message here to Gao Family Village, asking Liu Nineteen to 'pray at their Militia's shrine' – he wanted to take the opportunity to get rid of him. Anyway, Liu Nineteen killed the lot of them, and he had all of the Shi family's grain stores and fodder handed out to his own men. That coup allowed him to set up a mobile artillery unit. Liu Nineteen is very quick on the uptake, and he's absolutely ruthless. He's the number one in the Qian Division of the Militia of Righteous Harmony."

"Is he from Gao Family Village?"

"No. He's from somewhere in Shandong. He only arrived in Gao Family Village in the spring of this year."

"What about Elder Brother and Third Brother then?"

"I don't know. That was the first time I ever set eyes on either of them."

"I don't understand their names. Who are all of these brothers? That one called 'Elder Brother', could he be the Liu Nineteen you've been telling me about?"

"Oh, no, quite impossible!" the thin man said. "Who gets to see Liu Nineteen straight off the bat? We're nobodies, right? Liu Nineteen isn't going to be interrogating us himself! Besides which, the leaders of the Militia of Righteous Harmony aren't called 'brothers' – they are 'masters'. The master here is Liu Nineteen – I've heard his real name is Liu Chengxiang. The heads of each gang under a master are called brothers. According to how senior they are, they are called Elder Brother, Second Brother, Third Brother and so on."

"What does Liu Nineteen look like?"

"I have no idea. All I know is that he's nineteen years old. That's why everyone calls him Liu Nineteen."

"How could a nineteen-year-old be so powerful?" Ouyang Jue exclaimed in surprise.

"Everyone says he's the nearest thing to Liu Bowen – a natural-born military genius. Apparently, if you shoot at him, it's just like shooting at a brick wall – he doesn't even move a muscle."

"Can that possibly be true? It sounds quite incredible! You seem to know a lot about it."

When the thin man heard that, he spoke with even more energy. But the louder his voice got, the hoarser it became, as if something in his throat were broken. "I've heard other people speak of even more amazing things than that," he said. "You have to believe it. He came here to the Gao Family Village this spring to make this place the headquarters of his division. As soon as he arrived here, more than ten thousand Boxers came to join him from Qingyun, Yanshan and Dezhou – every village west of Tianjin, big and small, has been taken over by his men. If he didn't have magic spells to keep them safe, who would risk their lives in following him?"

"What does he look like? Is he really impressive-looking?"

"I've never heard anyone mention what he looks like. I come from over by the Danan River, and what I heard was that when the head of our Boxers, Han Yili, came over to Gao Family Village to pray at the Militia's shrine here, Liu Nineteen had a red cloth wound round his face so all you could see was his eyes."

"Is he afraid of other people seeing him? Why would that be?"

"Didn't I tell you just now that there are loads of people who want him dead? He's worried someone will try to assassinate him!"

Ouyang Jue thought that quite bizarre, and said, "Doesn't he have spells to keep him safe? Why should he be afraid of being assassinated?"

"I wouldn't know about that, but he's definitely not afraid of death. I've heard that he's always right there on the front line of every battle. The foreigners' rifles and cannons can't hurt him."

"Really?"

"The Westerners are all scared witless of him. We aren't too far from the Foreign Concession here, but they would never dare set foot in Gao Family Village. Hitara Hala Yulu, the governor of Zhili Province, has a lot of respect for him too. I've heard that the first time he met him, he gave him a bay horse – a really fabulous animal."

In the darkness, neither man could see the other. Ouyang Jue could only hear the thin man's hoarse voice. The things he told him were the stuff of dreams; he'd never seen or heard of anything like it. However, it did not matter whether he believed a word of it or not – this was now the world he lived in too.

A few days earlier, he had been entirely caught up in a wonderful, fantastical relationship with Xénia, but now all of a sudden he had fallen headlong into this absurd and bizarre situation. It was impossible… unimaginable! However, the things that had happened between himself and Xénia he had experienced for himself, while what he knew of Liu Nineteen was only what the thin man had told him. He was a little sceptical as to the truth of what the thin man had said; it might well be all invention. "I live in the old city," he explained, "so I really had no idea about what was going on out here. I can't understand it – why is this a completely different world from the old city? What you've been telling me about… did you see this with your own eyes, or is this just gossip you've picked up?"

"I'm about to have my head hacked off any moment now – do you really think I'm going to be trying to mess you around? If your city is taken over by the Boxers, you'll find everything is different there too! Just think about it – the Militia of Righteous Harmony arrived in Tianjin a couple of months ago from Shandong and Hebei. Now every village has set up a Militia shrine, and everyone's busy practising boxing. They all want to be possessed by the gods when they fight so they'll be invulnerable. It's like the flood has come, and we've all been engulfed by the waves. Why else would you be locked up here? Do you think Elder Brother and Third Brother are also just gossip I've picked up?"

Ouyang Jue was left speechless. He began to wonder what should he do. Was he really going to die here? Was there any way for him to get out of this alive? What more strange things would happen to him? In the past couple of months, he had experienced more than in the previous twenty-plus years put together, and it had all been strange, absurd, wonderful and terrible. But thinking about it, right now he remained most concerned about his family back in the old city and Xénia in the Foreign Concession – two different sets of people with nothing to do with each other. To one side, Xénia would be waiting for him; but over on the other side, there were his father, Shuxian and his elder brother: he'd suddenly disappeared, and they must be searching for him desperately. Would he ever see them again?

He felt as if he were falling into a bottomless pit, tumbling deeper and deeper, but unable to grasp anything that could save him. Feeling utterly helpless, he sighed and said despairingly, "I think I'd rather be dead than live like this!"

The thin man's reply was even more despairing. Coldly, he said, "Well, it's me they are going to kill."

The thin man was right: the following day, they came and took him away. No one in his village was prepared to vouch for him, so in accordance with the Militia's rules he was dragged out and beheaded. As to whether he really was a spy – who could say? Once he was dead, only Yama, King of Hell, would know if he was innocent or not. Although Ouyang Jue had spent a couple of days in the thin man's company, given that it was so dark that he could not see his hand in front of his face, all that was left to him was the memory of that hoarse voice and the kindness he'd shown when his simple medical skills had helped him to recover from his abdominal pains. He thanked him from the bottom of his heart. Besides, the thin man had told him a lot of things he needed to know so that he could understand the precariousness of the bizarre situation in which he found himself. His advice had served to warn him, and helped him... maybe even saved his life.

Now Ouyang Jue was left alone, squatting in one corner of that dark room.

A few days later, the door was suddenly flung open again and Third Brother's bulky figure loomed out at him from a dazzling shaft of light. "Can you keep accounts?" he demanded.

Ouyang Jue was flummoxed for a moment by being asked a question like this out of the blue. "My family is in business, so of course I can keep accounts."

"Come with me," Third Brother said.

He struggled to his feet. When he stood up, he couldn't stand straight, and by the time he'd got himself upright he couldn't walk because his body was shaking so badly, not to mention the fact that his left knee was still extremely painful. Shaking and limping, he followed Third Brother out of the room. He found it difficult to bear the strong light out of doors. He had been locked inside a pitch-black room for many days, and his eyes were blinded now that he had at long last emerged. He was trying his best to maintain his balance so that he didn't fall down; at the same time, he narrowed his eyes into tiny slits as he forced himself to keep up with Third Brother and follow him over to the other end of the yard, where he went through a small door. The light inside the room was dim, and much more comfortable for his eyes. "You'll be working under Zhu San in keeping our accounts," Third Brother said. "Just do what he tells you."

Ouyang Jue gradually made out a man sitting opposite him: nearly fifty years old, with a long sallow face, tiny deep-set eyes, thin pale lips, and long hairs curling out of his nostrils, like the rank weeds poking out from the mouth of a disused well. He was wearing a ragged, patched jacket with a blue turban tied round his head; his expression was irritable and unfriendly. When they came in, he was writing up his accounts at a small wooden table. Lying on the table, there was a broken abacus and a stone inkstone, as well as heaps of account books.

Third Brother was quick and decisive in everything he did. He told Zhu San, "Take good care of him, and make sure he knows the rules. Every evening, someone will come and escort him back to the stables." Then he turned around and walked away as fast as he could.

Zhu San sat down and told him to stand there and listen. Speaking in a reproachful tone, he explained the very strict rules that pertained here one by one, and then he asked, "Can you remember everything I've told you?" Zhu San spoke with an obvious rural accent. He must come from one of the villages out to the south of the city.

Ouyang Jue was an educated young man, and he was rather clever. He immediately summed up Zhu San's rules in the words of the *Analects of Confucius*: "See no evil; hear no evil; do no evil."

But that kind of cleverness was useless here. It just annoyed Zhu San, and he shouted at him, "What on earth are you on about? Keep your head down and do your job. Don't ask any questions about what is going on around the shrine. Stay right here in this room and don't go anywhere – in fact, if you set foot outside this courtyard without permission, I'll break your legs for you. What kind of moron are you that you can't even remember that? Do you need me to say them over again for a third time?"

Ouyang Jue quickly repeated what Zhu San had said word for word, and he was satisfied. He wasn't sure what Third Brother intended to do with him; however, his priority right now was staying alive. He was desperate to know if Third Brother had sent someone over to the old city to check on him, but he couldn't possibly ask. This was something that the thin man had told him, and Third Brother had never so much as mentioned it. Now he'd been set to work keeping accounts, so at least that meant they weren't planning to kill him in the short term. He might yet survive as long as he did his bookkeeping well, made them happy and convinced them that he was useful.

Ouyang Jue realised that Zhu San might seem difficult to deal with, but in fact he was just a peasant, and his abilities were strictly limited. All he needed to do was to help Zhu San do his job well, while telling everyone else that this was all Zhu San's work, to make sure that he couldn't do without him. That way, he might hope to get out of this alive. Ouyang Jue had never given a thought to how to deal with other people before, but needs must; he had to negotiate his relationship with this man very carefully.

His job was to keep accounts for the warehouses. This was a huge complex. There was a little hut out front for the ledgers, and behind that were a series of large storehouses where stuff was kept. These used to be granaries owned by a wealthy local family. However, these people were second-class hairys, and the moment Liu Nineteen arrived they took to their heels. Now, their granaries served this Boxer division as a place to store military equipment and provisions.

Every day, it was Ouyang Jue's task to follow Zhu San around as he recorded everything entering and leaving the warehouses. At the end of each day, the figures from each of the account books had to be reported to Third Brother. It seemed that Third Brother managed things in much the same way as his own elder brother, Ouyang Zun, at the paper shop. Everything had to be set out in detail so he could see at a glance exactly where he stood. The items they registered included all kinds of things: clothing, weapons, food, medicine, various trophies captured during the fighting, as well as all the necessities for the proper burial of Militia members killed in battle, and so on. Every day, vast quantities of things had to be logged as they went in and out. Zhu San was quite frankly struggling – though admittedly even if he'd been a great deal more competent than he was, one person would find it hard to keep on top of this avalanche. Ouyang Jue was working very hard, and it was exhausting. In the past, he'd spent his days messing around with a little dilettante painting and calligraphy – he wasn't used to the world of work. Having laboured from morning until night for a few days, he was feeling shattered, and what is more his leg still wasn't right, so he was limping along as awkwardly as a barrow with a wonky wheel. But if he wanted to survive, this was what he had to do.

Each time the Boxers went out to fight, the storehouse would be busy for a while. Sometimes they were issuing dozens of cases of broadswords and rifles, along with cartloads of gunpowder and hay. When they returned victorious from the fight, there would be wagon upon wagon of loot brought back to the warehouses that needed to be logged, and more would have come back than had been issued in the first place. Ouyang Jue was just responsible for keeping accounts – he had nothing to do with loading and unloading. He wasn't allowed to deal with the guns or materiel, and as a matter of fact, he wouldn't have dared to so much as touch them.

For the first few days, Ouyang Jue was fetched from the stable by Zhu San every morning and was escorted back by one of the Boxers in the evening. Since he was busy all day every day, this soon became exhausting. But after a couple of days of this routine, Ouyang Jue realised that he was beginning to recover from his ordeal. The main reason for this was that since starting work in the warehouse, he was eating three square meals like the rest of them – they were getting cornmeal flatbreads, vegetable stew and hot soup. Once he was having enough to eat, he felt so much better. All living creatures depend on food.

Since he was now eating properly, his mental state also improved. Although he had laid down strict rules for himself along the lines of don't listen, don't look, don't ask, don't touch, he was secretly observing his environment with close attention. He could see that this Boxer division was very well organised, with a clear chain of command, but also that these men remained on high alert and were capable of extreme violence. He realised that the whole place was strictly guarded and there were sentries patrolling everywhere – each building had Militia members posted on the roof, so there was absolutely nowhere to hide. If you tried to run, you would be spotted immediately. The thin man was right. "Even if you grew a pair of wings, you wouldn't be able to get out of here!"

These people seldom talked to each other; no one cracked a joke or smoked a pipe, and none of them ever drank alcohol. Ouyang Jue happened to hear someone say that not long after they first arrived in the spring, Second Brother went over to Heiniucheng to fight a bunch of second-class hairys. On the way back, when he stopped for dinner, he drank a pot of wine. When he came back, Liu Nineteen smelled the alcohol on his breath, and he'd personally given him ten strokes of the cane. His back had been cut to ribbons, and for the next couple of weeks he'd had to sleep on his stomach.

Around the Militia shrine, there were sword blades everywhere, shining in the sunlight. When these people encountered each other, they would salute with one hand to their chest and then give a secret password. The words they used were very strange. One of them would ask, "Who is your guarantor?" Then, the other person had to reply, "A disciple." Ouyang Jue had no idea what it all meant. Gradually, he came to realise that for all that this village was the headquarters of the division, the Brothers lived elsewhere. As for where their leader, Liu Nineteen, was living, nobody knew, and he wasn't going to ask. The ordinary Boxers camped, practised and cast their spells outside the courtyard where Ouyang Jue was confined. The walls of the courtyard were so high that he could not see outside. From within the courtyard, he could sometimes hear the Boxers stamping their feet as they practised outside – that was the *pok... pok...* sound he'd noticed when he first arrived. When they stamped in unison, the sound was so loud that the ground seemed to shake. He could only imagine just how many Boxers it needed to make a noise like that, and he was caught in the middle of it all as securely as if they'd imprisoned him in an iron cage.

He didn't even try to run away; it was impossible.

Of course, he was desperate to escape – he was desperate to see Xénia again after being separated for so many days. He couldn't see her, but he could imagine the expression in her beautiful, deep-blue eyes as she waited for him far away. One night, he woke himself up by shouting. Once he came to, he was scared to death by his own yelling. He didn't know what he had been shouting about. Fortunately, no one heard. But then he thought: it's so quiet here at night, and there are sentries posted on the roof and out in the yard – of course they must have heard something! Or did his screaming exist only in his own mind, and he actually hadn't made a sound?

He had to control himself. Staying alive was his first consideration now. A terrible reality forced him to be realistic.

CHAPTER 10

During the Boxers' heyday, Qing officers and soldiers swelled their ranks

ONCE IT GOT to the middle of May, the city was being faced with a new crisis every single day.

An endless stream of Boxers were pouring into the north-western part of the old city from Shandong and Hebei, wearing red, yellow, blue or purple headscarves or turbans – flooding into Tianjin from the direction of the Grand Canal. Some came marching in an orderly line, their banners and flags held high, looking like military units; others looked more like renegade soldiers or mercenaries, and they were completely undisciplined. Sometimes, these men came in small groups, armed with swords or clubs – wandering about aimlessly, they nevertheless invested the scene with a threatening aura. Wherever they went, Christians fled. But as everyone was well aware, the Boxers had come to fight the foreign troops garrisoned over in Tianjin's Zhizhulin Concession. By this time, the Westerners had already gained control of the Dagu Forts, so their warships could sail directly to Zizhulin up the White River.

The Militia of Righteous Harmony was organised in accordance with the Eight Trigrams. Outsiders might not know which division an individual belonged to, but the Boxers themselves could tell at a glance. They would know immediately if someone belonged to the Qian Division, the Kan Division or the Li Division, and who the master was; just like in a group of sparrows, the birds themselves know exactly who nests with whom. The vast majority of the Militia's foot-soldiers were farmers, fishermen, blacksmiths, boatman, peddlers, labourers, coolies, vagrants or beggars. No one had issued them with uniforms, so they wore their usual vests and trousers. The weather was already hot, and these people were used to stripping off, showing torsos burned black by many years of working under the sun. They wore cloth shoes on their feet, and occasionally you would even see someone in straw sandals. Those kitted out in straw sandals would usually have a few new pairs hanging from their belts in case the ones they were wearing got worn out. Although these fierce warriors assembling from all directions were dressed in completely different kinds of clothing, they couldn't hide their true identities from the people of Tianjin whose wits had been sharpened by growing up on the wharfs – they were used to seeing all kinds of people from every part of the country. They quickly got the hang of identifying which division a particular Boxer belonged to by looking at the different colours of the turbans and sashes they wore.

By the second week of May, most of the Militia of Righteous Harmony's rank and file who had arrived in Tianjin still remained outside the walls, quietly setting up camp and waiting for the moment to strike. At that time, there were some strong military units stationed in Tianjin, most notably the Front Division of the Wuwei Army under the command of Nie Shicheng. They were well-equipped and armed with foreign-made guns.

Up until this point, the government had been determined to put down the 'Boxer Rebellion', and they'd announced a shoot-to-kill policy. However, recently this had changed: one faction at court wanted to exterminate the 'Boxer bandits', but another wanted to use these fearless fighters to put pressure on the increasingly troublesome Westerners – maybe they could even kick them out entirely. The foreigners were counting on the might of their ships and artillery, but the Boxers proclaimed that they were possessed by spirits, and therefore no gun could hurt them. There was no consensus at court on the issue: some said that the Boxers' claims of invulnerability were nothing but a pack of lies, but others believed every word. The Empress Dowager and the Guangxu Emperor could not agree, and the senior ministers were in even greater disarray. With such deep divisions at the heart of government, cracks began to open in the system. This gave the Boxer toughs room to manoeuvre.

There was a terrible drought in Gengzi year – 1900 according to the Western calendar – so the farmers had nothing to do. In drought years, the political situation is always volatile; naturally, they now turned their anger against the colonial powers who in recent years had proved only too eager to carve up the Qing regime. The Boxer Rebellion was like a wildfire, blazing up wherever the wind blew, and now those winds had blown them as far as Tianjin, where they planned to fight to the death against the foreigners. In recent days, like a plague of locusts, vast numbers of

Militia foot-soldiers had gathered outside the city, and there was absolutely nothing the government could do to stop them.

On the seventeenth of May, some people set up a Boxer shrine outside the Temple to the Three Heroes. As soon as news reached the local magistrate, he immediately sent soldiers to move them on by force. The next day, an even bigger group of Militia members arrived to make a show of strength – there were a bunch of men using broadswords to mark out an area of the courtyard in front of the Temple to the Three Heroes. The sharp blades of broadswords threw sparks as they scraped across the stone paving slabs, leaving deep scratches. Afterwards, they proceeded to the main gate, where they recited spells and summoned the spirits to possess them. One of these possessed Brothers rolled up his sleeves and picked up a three-inch-thick slab of stone that he smashed against the crown of his head. With a sharp crack, the stone slab broke, while his head was uninjured. Hearing about this is nothing – seeing it with your own eyes is everything! Now people really believed that the Boxers had supernatural abilities, and their shrine was erected immediately.

As soon as they had successfully taken over the Temple to the Three Heroes, rioting broke out inside and outside the city walls. Three churches were torched – the one in front of the magistrate's office inside the old city; the one by the West Gate; and the one over by the main entrance to the government granary. Afterwards, an even more daring group went over to the mouth of the Three Rivers and burned the Church of Notre-Dame des Victoires to the ground. Now there was nobody who would dare to try to put out a fire in a church – once it started burning, the flames just spread and spread. That night, the sky stayed bright long after the sun had set. Many people climbed the city walls to watch the fires burning.

Thirty years before, in the ninth year of the reign of the Tongzhi Emperor, the residents of Tianjin had torched the Church of Notre-Dame des Victoires during anti-Christian riots provoked by rumours that the nuns there were murdering Chinese children – the appalling violence that followed had horrified the entire world. When order was restored, any number of rioters had been executed, but this merely served to entrench the enmity the people of Tianjin felt for the Western powers. Now, thirty years later, this ill-fated church was on fire again, and the flames were burning even brighter. Onlookers watched the fire just as they might enjoy the fireworks on New Year's Eve. At this time, the inhabitants of the old city were trying to establish their credentials as anti-foreign and anti-Christian – they didn't spare a thought for how the people over in Zizhulin would view their actions.

The following day, Cao Futian, the leader of the Kan Division, advanced at the head of thousands of Militia members as they went from Jinghai to the Lü Dongbin Daoist monastery in the north-western part of the city, where they set up an altar, arranged an impressive display of swords and rifles, and then burned incense and cast magic spells. This was now his headquarters. Even more to the point, Zhang Decheng marched his notorious 'Number One Division' from the township of Duliu right into the old city of Tianjin, establishing his headquarters just inside the walls by the Xiaoyi Gate. When Zhang Decheng rode into the city, all kinds of colourful battle-standards with serrated edges came flooding through the city gate. At the same time, the people of the city were kneeling down on both sides of the road, welcoming them with the greatest respect. The Militia of Righteous Harmony was now in charge of Tianjin. With Master Zhang and Master Cao in place, not to mention Master Liu Nineteen down south, the Boxers had total control of the city.

The Xiaoyi Gate stood only a few hundred metres away from Old Master Ouyang's house on Fushu Street. If Zhang Decheng mobilised his men, the Ouyang family could hear it loud and clear.

Thinking over the events of the last couple of days, the Boxers seemed to have come from nowhere – almost as if someone had been sowing dragon's teeth. In the blink of an eye, they were all over the city. The 'Number One Division' always wore red; right across the city, every lane and alley was a sea of red. For some reason this reminded Old Master Ouyang of the 'hanged-man' caterpillars that had suddenly appeared the year before, followed by the big black crows that flew in from who-knows-where. The night that the three churches in the city burned down, the conflagration shot bright red flames high into the sky, and even as he sat in his living room he could see the fires. This reminded him of the old scholar tree suddenly catching fire on New Year's Eve the year before. This time, he thought, we really are in for it.

Tianjin has always been a peculiar place. Normally, it seems entirely peaceful. On the surface, everything is perfectly harmonious; people go out to eat and drink; they go shopping; and they are out and about having fun. But this city is built on land reclaimed from the sea: the earth is salty, and the water is brackish... even the air has a bitter tang. These qualities have entered the blood of its people. Once established in their blood, their temper, character, likes and dislikes, tastes, ways of doing things and lifestyle will be different from those of folk from other places. What is found in their eyes, their minds and their bones is also different from the qualities other people possess. What they are interested in, what they care about and the things they get up to are also different from what you would see in other places. As a result, although Tianjin might seem to be a perfectly ordinary city, it is a place that produces remarkable men and women, and many tales of great deeds. As these spread by word of mouth, they become even more amazing. So, once the Boxer Rebellion began, all kinds of myths and legends circulated, becoming more bizarre at every turn.

After the Boxers entered the city, the Yellow Lotus Divine Matriarch also arrived in Tianjin. She came by boat along the Grand Canal. She anchored her boat, hung with red lanterns, where the canal skirted the Houjiahou red-light district; this was her headquarters. The women of Tianjin rushed there to have a look, fighting to join the Red Lanterns Militia, with the same enthusiasm as they showed for the annual festival for the Queen of Heaven on the twenty-third of March. Dressed in bright red shirts and trousers, they went swaggering through the markets. Every three days, the all-female Red Lanterns Militia entered the old city to march through the streets. A couple of thousand women dressed from head to foot in red entered via the North Gate, walked once around the Drum Tower, and then tramped away. Each of them was armed with a sword, and their faces were veiled. In addition, every woman carried a red lantern and a fan. They shouted in unison:

Women don't comb their hair; they cut off foreigners' heads!
Women don't bind their feet; they laugh to see the
  foreigners dead!

At that moment, it seemed as though the entire city of Tianjin had gone crazy. It was unimaginable, and yet it was happening right in front of their eyes.

Mrs Jiang, the Ouyang family's cook, went out to buy onions, whereupon she was stopped by two women wearing red who wanted her to join the Red Lanterns. Mrs Jiang refused, saying that she was too old. The two women in red asked her how old she was and if she was married. That was when she discovered that the women's Militia wasn't restricted to the Red Lanterns. Middle-aged women were enrolled in the Blue Lanterns, while widows joined the Black Lanterns. Old women were called Pot Lanterns because they were employed to cook for the Boxers. They tried to drag Mrs Jiang over to the nearest Boxer shrine to sign her up. She was so scared that she just dropped her onions and ran all the way home. After that, she did not dare go out again – she sent Zhang Yi to do the shopping.

For the Ouyang family, it was one shock after another.

One day, they heard shouting; people were yelling that the Boxers had set fire to the outer wall of the house. Zhang Yi ran out to have a look, and sure enough, flames were licking the tops of the wall the whole way round the house. It was a terrifying sight. When he looked more closely, it turned out someone had set fire to the paper-collection baskets hanging from the walls. At that time, there was a custom in Tianjin that in order to show respect for the written word – for culture – locals would hang up bamboo baskets on the walls of their houses with a strip of paper pasted above, reading, "Respect the Written Word". This was to remind people that if they happened to see a piece of paper on the ground with something written on it, they should pick it up and put it in one of these baskets. When Old

Master Ouyang came to Tianjin for the first time, he admired this practice very much. He said that this kind of cherishing the written word had long been the custom in the Yangtze River delta region too, and that since the Ouyang family was in the paper business, they had more reason than most to show their respect. Thus, they had hung two baskets on each side of the outer wall, and over the course of the next twenty years, they had come to be an indispensable part of the refined way of life carried on in this old house. But now some unpleasant little bastard had decided to set light to them. Seeing that it was just a nasty prank, Zhang Yi immediately took down the burning wastepaper baskets and put the fires out. It was just a false alarm, but the walls seemed terribly bare without their baskets. Old Master Ouyang looked at them and sighed, but all he said was, "In troubled times, there is no place for good manners."

On another day, someone came to the Ouyang house and banged on the door, saying that the Boxers were going over to Zizhulin to set fire to the foreign buildings there. They were ordered to prepare forty-eight 'Victory' sesame-stuffed cakes and eight buckets of sweet mung-bean soup to treat the members of the Militia when they returned in triumph. Once this had been done and it was all ready, nobody came to collect it. The weather was really hot by this time, and none of the Ouyang family felt much like eating, so these huge cakes made with expensive white flour and all of that mung-bean soup ended up going to waste. Two days after that, a couple of Boxers with red turbans wrapped round their heads came to the door to demand money. Zhang Yi gave them some silver to get rid of them, but thinking about it afterwards, he felt that he recognised some of those faces – then he remembered that they belonged to that bunch of petty criminals who hung out near the Baiyi Nunnery; they were endlessly causing trouble. The following day, things took a turn for the worse. Someone kept slapping the door with the flat of his hand until they opened up – as hard and fast as if he were practising 'Iron Palm' boxing – and when they did, they saw a group of people standing there who wanted to use their front courtyard as a Boxer shrine. This terrified the entire household. For the next few days, they were frightened of anyone knocking on the door. When someone called, their hearts would start pounding as if their last hour had come. Luckily, those people went away and never came back. As to why they didn't return, who could say?

Outside the house, chaos reigned. Boxer shrines were everywhere. Some locals had also hung up flags and put out altars. There were all sorts of incomers who'd set up their own – it was very confusing and impossible to tell real from fake. The eldest young master came up with two strategies to deal with the situation. First, he asked Zhang Yi to wrap a length of red cloth around his head, and if anyone asked he was to pretend that he'd joined the Militia of Righteous Harmony. That way, in future, people would leave them alone. This worked really well: if anyone turned up claiming to be a Boxer, Zhang Yi would go out to meet them with his red turban on. He was a big man, and with his turban wrapped round his head he really did look just like a Boxer. It did not matter whether the other party was really a member of the Militia or not; they weren't going to be making any demands. His second strategy was to stick a piece of red paper right by the front door, with the words "Victory to the Fists of Righteous Harmony" written on it. At this time, lots of the rich families in the old city were doing the same in the hope of avoiding trouble. However, in the past, it would have been the second young master who did this kind of writing; now, Old Master Ouyang had to write it himself. When Old Master Ouyang picked up his brush, he couldn't help bursting into tears.

For more than two weeks now, there had been no word from the missing second young master, and the Ouyang family was in a panic. There was only one thing on their minds: they had to find the second young master! But the more they searched, the more baffling it became. How could a grown man just disappear like that? Old Master Ouyang had lived in Tianjin for more than twenty years, and he'd never heard of anyone vanishing all of a sudden. The old master had called every single staff member of the Gongnan paper shop to the house for questioning without getting anything useful out of them. Only one thing that Wei Xiaosan said caught his attention. He said that since the second young master had started working at the Gongnan Avenue store, he mostly only turned up in the afternoon and was hardly ever there in the morning. Old Master Ouyang thought that there might be something in this: his son had set off for the Gongnan shop after breakfast every day, so if he hadn't gone there directly, where did he go instead? Maybe he thought it was boring being in the shop and so he'd snuck off to meet his painter friends every morning? Old Master Ouyang sent someone to question the second young master's closest friends, but they all said they hadn't seen him. The second young master's social circle had always been quite limited, so his family did the rounds of the academies and ateliers, bookstores and antique shops that he would visit from time to time, but everyone just shook their heads and said they hadn't seen him. It was all most peculiar – after all, he couldn't just have vanished into thin air.

Every member of the household proffered ideas to Old Master Ouyang with the exception of two people. One was the eldest young master, and the other was Shuxian. Both of them knew something about what had been going on, and they had their own views on the subject, but they couldn't speak. However, what they knew was different, so what they thought had happened was different too.

The eldest young master knew the most. He'd even seen the French woman concerned. He knew that his second brother was as one possessed, and he felt sure that his disappearance must be connected in some way with that foreign woman. But that day over on Guyi Street, he'd been so angry with his brother – would he dare to go back to the Foreign Concession to meet her again? His brother was so well-educated, he ought to understand... surely all of this reading could not have completely addled his head? Did he really want to die for love like Liang Shanbo? But if he hadn't gone out to the Foreign Concession, that would mean he'd disappeared somewhere in the old city! The situation was already extremely dangerous, and the Westerners were spoiling for a fight. If he'd really gone over to the Foreign Concession, the chances were that he'd been arrested by them. If he'd fallen into the hands of her father... well, he was an officer in the French Army – he would just kill him...

Thinking about this, he felt appalled, the chill spreading across his body. He regretted slapping his brother across the face that day.

At the time, he couldn't imagine where his strength came from – he could have snapped a plank with his bare hands! They'd got on so well together for more than twenty years, and he'd never laid a hand on him before, but now he could still feel the sensation of hitting his palm against his brother's smooth face... that made him feel awful! Had his slap succeeded in making him break up with the foreign woman, or did it make him feel they had to be together whatever the cost? Why hadn't he dragged him home afterwards or found someplace to lock him up? But there was no point saying anything about it now. He was furious with himself: he'd failed his brother, he'd failed his father and Shuxian. The last few days, in fact, he had been hiding from the rest of the family all the efforts he was making to find his younger brother, but from first to last there was no news. The only explanation seemed to be that he was being held inside the Foreign Concession.

He kept warning himself not to say a word about the French woman. If Shuxian found out about that, it would kill her.

However, he was amazed to discover that of all the family members, it was Shuxian who seemed most unfazed by the disappearance of the second young master. On the surface, she carried on exactly as before. She never discussed it with anyone else, nor was she hysterically sending people to all manner of unlikely places to look for her husband. What she worried about was Father's mood; sometimes she would go to Father's living room to sit with him and listen to his wild surmises. Sometimes she might break in and say a few words, something to calm his burning anxiety. The eldest young master thought to himself that by refusing to panic and putting all her efforts into cheering up an unhappy old man, his sister-in-law really was showing her sterling qualities. His own Xifeng couldn't begin to compare!

However, as time passed, the day came when he realised that his sister-in-law was getting thinner and thinner, to the point where the tendons in her neck were standing proud and there were obvious bags under her eyes. Now he started to pay attention, he realised she clearly wasn't eating properly. It's hard to hide gnawing anxieties for any length of time. He quietly advised her, "Don't worry, Shuxian, I've been sending people out to look for him. With the chaos out there, it's not surprising that people get into trouble. However, he's so clever, no matter what happens to him, he will find a way to look after himself."

At the moment of speaking, he and Shuxian were on their way out of Father's courtyard, and there was no one else around them. Shuxian suddenly whispered, "Can I ask you to do something for me?"

"There's no need to be so polite," Ouyang Zun said. "If there's anything I can do to help, just let me know."

Zhuang Shuxian hesitated for a moment and then said, "Have you thought about searching for him in places like Houjiahou?" She spoke lightly, as if she were just chatting, and her expression never changed a jot.

The eldest young master was shocked. He had no idea that her thoughts had been running in that direction! Clearly, she knew that her husband's disappearance was concerned with a woman, but she obviously did not know about the French girl because she seemed to think that he was involved in an affair with a whore in one of the Houjiahou brothels. The eldest young master thought Shuxian must have spotted that something was going on. She's known for ages that the second young master was being unfaithful to her. If Xifeng had been in her shoes, wouldn't the whole house have been in an uproar all this time? More than ever, he admired Shuxian's tolerance and composure. She didn't just do this for her own sake, to preserve her own self-respect, but also to save face for the Ouyang family. He was very moved but had no idea how to express it, so he comforted her in a low voice. "I've considered that – in fact, I'm in the process of looking into it. Leave it to me – I will get him back!"

Zhuang Shuxian just said in measured way, "Do be careful, and don't let anyone else know."

Ouyang Zun was far from stupid. "I understand," he said. "I won't say a word to anyone – even in the family. Please don't worry."

Shuxian thanked him and quietly went back to her courtyard in the shadow of the great scholar tree.

Ouyang Zun was very clear about why Shuxian had spoken to

him the way she had; he must not allow Xifeng to know anything about what had happened to the second young master, nor any of the ideas and information they had about him. He knew that Xifeng had no ill intentions, but she was very curious and interfering, and she simply could not stop herself from gossiping. If someone like her got involved in something the least bit sensitive, they would only make it worse. The day before, Xifeng had gone to visit Shuxian at home. She wasn't intending to gossip; she just thought that poor Shuxian must be anxious and lonely, and might like some company. When she came through the door, she saw her sitting there, peeling some melon seeds. "Don't you always keep your melon seeds in that little celadon jar?" she asked. "Why are you using a baluster vase instead?"

Shuxian immediately got up and asked her to sit down. "Since the second young master hasn't come back, the little jar is full. Now I'm putting them in here. Besides, I've got nothing else to do, and I'm used to it. If you'd like to have some, take them away with you."

"Keep them for him," Xifeng said. "I guess he'll be back any day now. A grown man can't just disappear, so sooner or later he'll turn up again."

Shuxian smiled and didn't say a word. She just carried on peeling her seeds.

"I can't imagine where he can possibly have gone…" Xifeng said. "He didn't say a word to his brother, nor to Father, but he surely would have said something to you…"

Xifeng's words wiped the smile off Shuxian's face, but she still didn't speak. Instead, she kept on working away at the husks of the melon seeds. Xifeng was far too insensitive to notice a thing.

Xifeng suddenly swung round and cracked what she thought was a hilarious joke. "I do hope he hasn't run off with another woman!" She looked teasingly at Shuxian and started to giggle.

Shuxian stopped dead and doubled up in a violent coughing fit, choking and hacking, her face as white as a sheet. It seemed as though something was terribly wrong. Xifeng was scared witless and screamed for Mrs Jiang. Fortunately, ever since Ouyang Jue disappeared, Old Master Ouyang had told Mrs Jiang to stick close to Shuxian whenever she had a free moment, to make sure someone was there with her. When Mrs Jiang heard Xifeng shouting, she came running as quickly as she could. She realised that Shuxian had managed to get a melon-seed husk stuck in her throat, so she immediately crumbled up some lumps of steamed bread and got Shuxian to swallow them, washed down with a cup of tea. This method worked very well. In a trice, the melon-seed husk was pushed down her throat and into her stomach.

After it was all over, she coughed twice, bringing up a mouthful of phlegm flecked with a little blood.

Mrs Jiang had no idea how Zhuang Shuxian could have come to do such a thing. She had been peeling melon seeds for the second young master for years now, and nothing had ever got caught in her throat before. Of course, Xifeng didn't realise that her joke had been a stab to Shuxian's heart – she genuinely believed that Ouyang Jue had disappeared because he'd run off with another woman.

Only Ouyang Zun knew something of the pain this unhappy woman was hiding. Now, it was up to him to help her by finding the second young master as quickly as possible.

This morning, the Ouyang family had been woken by the *boom... boom* of a cannon bombardment. Some people were shouting that the foreigners were shelling the city; others were running through the streets and lanes screaming that Master Zhang was casting a spell to protect them, telling every family to hang up a red lantern each night and that during the day they should stuff the chimney in the roof with cloths stained with menstrual blood because this would block the Westerners' guns.

Zhang Yi asked Old Master Ouyang what to do. Old Master Ouyang came from Zhejiang Province; he was an educated gentleman who respected the teachings of Confucius and never had any time for belief in supernatural forces or magical powers, let alone the kind of mumbo jumbo that periodically swept through Tianjin. He said that they should hang a red lantern over the door every night, but he had no intention of asking his daughters-in-law to hang the cloths they used during their periods up on the roof in broad daylight. Besides, over the last few days, the sound of gunfire had always come from outside the city walls. The army had obviously joined forces with the Boxers to fight the colonial powers, but this was all happening outside the city. Depending on who you asked, the fighting was taking place in various different locations: one day they claimed it was happening by the Beiyang Army gun foundry; the next day it was over at the Xigu Arsenal; and the day after that it was the Tientsin Military Academy – all of them quite a way away from the old city. Besides which, the Qing Army had their own guns, and it was impossible to know exactly who was firing. In the past, the residents of Tianjin rarely heard the sound of artillery, but now day after day the *boom... boom...* of the guns sounded constantly, frightening everyone out of their wits. They seemed to spend the whole day on tenterhooks, but so far not a single shell had fallen inside the walls.

At present, most of the businesses in and around Tianjin had closed their doors, apart from the ones that sold food and drink. The Ouyang family's two paper shops in Gongnan Avenue and Guyi Street had been boarded up for the past ten days. Most of the clerks in the shops hadn't gone anywhere; they stayed in the shop trying to keep the stock from going up in flames. If a fire got started, they'd need all the help they could get: a hundred and ten tons of paper would feed a really volcanic blaze. Every day, the eldest young master had to patrol between the two stores in the north and east of the city, while at the same time racking his brains for new places to search for his younger brother. Luckily, they had Zhang Yi back at the house; he could deal with anything that came up, and the red cloth wound round his head really worked a treat. Zhang Yi said to the eldest young master with a smile, "This red cloth really does work to ward off evil."

Later that day, the eldest young master came back from Guyi Street. Just as he was about to go through the door, two men came up behind him: one fat and one thin. They weren't dressed like Militia members, but the tall, thin man had a purple sash around his waist. Tianjin people were by now well aware of the fact that a purple sash was the insignia of the Li Division.

Without waiting for him to open his mouth, the fat man with a round face demanded, "Are you the eldest young master of the Ouyang family that runs paper shops?"

"I am," Ouyang Zun said. "Who are you? What do you want with me?"

"Do you want to see your brother?" the chubby, round-faced man asked him.

Ouyang Zun was surprised and asked, "Do you know where he is?"

"I don't have time to stand around chatting!" the fat man said. "If you want to see him, come with us!" He charged off without ever turning round to look back.

Ouyang Zun set off trotting meekly along behind them.

As he walked, he was wondering: Who are these people? What has my brother been up to that he's fallen into their hands? Judging by their accents, they're from Shandong, not Tianjin, and those sashes mean they must be Boxers. But we aren't Christians, so I don't see what my brother can have done to offend them. Did he venture out to the Foreign Concession again and they caught him? He simply could not understand it. So far, he hadn't seen hide nor hair of his brother, and he had no idea where these men were taking him.

Ouyang Zun followed behind these two figures – one fat and one thin – as they proceeded out of the North Gate, across the pontoon bridge and west along the river. All the way along, he could see that the river was packed full of boats, most of them secured to the bank by hawsers, with red lanterns hanging from their masts. Sometimes, these red lanterns were enormous; on other boats, there were strings of dozens of lanterns; and occasionally there were also forests of flags, together with a single huge battle-standard – that probably marked one of the Red Lanterns' shrines. The little watercraft that plied the river crossing didn't have masts, so they'd all hoisted up little globular red lanterns on the end of a bamboo pole. By this time, the sky was already dark, and these red lights – big and small, near and far – formed bright clusters like the stars of the Milky Way in a spectacular, bizarre scene.

There were lots of people out on the riverbank, but the vast majority of them were Boxers. The fat man and the thin one plunged into the crowds: not only did they not slow down, they even quickened their pace. He followed close behind for fear of losing them. After making their way through one crowd after another, by the time they got to the Northern Temple, the people were starting to thin out. After crossing a wooded area, where the old trees were leaning this way and that, they entered a small temple. He had never been to this temple before and had no idea what deity it might be dedicated to. There were some twenty or thirty lanterns hanging up around the temple, lighting up the courtyard and the main hall. A group of Boxers were standing around in the courtyard. They weren't dressed alike: some had turbans wrapped round their heads while others were bare-headed, with a queue hanging down their backs; some wore purple sashes, but there were two with yellow belts – it all looked most peculiar.

As soon as he set foot inside the hall, he heard a voice coming towards him, ladened with menace. "How much are you prepared to pay to get your brother back?"

That sounded like there'd been a kidnapping. With the lights inside the hall shining right in his eyes, he could not see the speaker. "Whatever you want," he said quickly. "Name your price. But first you've got to tell me where my brother is."

Most unexpectedly, the man replied, "I can't tell you that."

"Can I at least see him?"

"You pay the money, and we'll make sure you get to see him. We'll go and rescue your brother, but you have to pay the money over first. Otherwise, it's none of our business."

Ouyang Zun was confused. Were these people holding his brother captive or not? Did they really know where he was? What could have happened to him that these men would need to 'rescue' him? Ouyang Zun was not stupid, and he was determined to find out exactly what was going on. "How do you know my brother is missing?" he asked.

The man laughed at that, but before he could say another word, an incredible racket started up outside the hall. There was shouting, the sound of running footsteps, the clash of swords, and then a group of people burst in, screaming at the tops of their voices. They were holding blazing torches in their hands, and this lit up a crowd of Boxers wearing bright yellow turbans. One of them, a very impressive-looking man, was sporting a black beard and thick bushy eyebrows. He shouted at the people inside the hall, "Which division do you belong to?"

"The Li Division."

"Who is your master?"

"Master Pang." The voice that answered him was a little faint.

"What are the names of all the Brothers? Quickly!"

The man hesitated and stuttered.

"Another lot of motherfucking gangsters!" the bearded man snapped. "What hole have these bastards crawled out from that they have the gall to kit themselves out like they're the Militia? Arrest the lot of them, and we'll deal with them back at the Lü Dongbin monastery."

Straightaway the Boxers holding torches set to work, and the people in the hall were rounded up and marched off without anyone offering the slightest resistance. The man with the black beard walked over to have a look at Ouyang Zun and asked, "What are you doing here?"

Ouyang Zun explained.

"You've been very lucky," the man with the black beard said. "We arrived to sort this mess out just in the nick of time. These thugs would have kidnapped you if we hadn't turned up." After that, he gathered up his men, who were still shouting and screaming, and took them away. The eldest young master was left all alone in an empty temple, blazing with light.

Ouyang Zun learned the next day that the night before the Boxers had been cleaning house all over the city. Inside the walls, it was Master Zhang Decheng and his 'Number One Division' that was responsible for sorting out the situation, while in the north and east it was Master Cao Futian and his Kan Division. They had broken up many a fake Boxer group, not to mention criminal gangs masquerading as Boxers who were using the fear the Militia of Righteous Harmony inspired to rob people or extort money. Some people said that this was all done by 'second-class hairys', but in fact this was not true. Chinese Christians were living in a state of constant terror, thinking that they could be killed at any moment – they wouldn't dare do anything of the kind. Most of these people were local gangsters or thugs coming in from elsewhere, and they were just in it for the money. Supposedly, there was one old man with a long beard going round in Daoist robes with his hair flowing down to his shoulders. He claimed to be one hundred and eight years old, the reincarnation of Bodhidharma Laozu. He'd set up his own shrine behind the Skanda Buddhist Temple in the east part of the city where he taught people incantations and magical martial arts techniques. He said that this way they could eliminate misfortune and avoid disaster, but it was all done to extort money. He got caught by Zhang Decheng, who cleaved him in two, starting from the top of his head. Some people said that the old man used to have a fortune-telling booth over on Beidaguan Avenue, and his beard was nothing but a bit of sheep's wool glued onto his face. Others said that the old man was actually a foreign priest dressed up like that to disguise himself – the story just got more and more ridiculous. However, once the real Boxers had got rid of the fakes, the situation inside the city was a bit more stable, and the wild rumours and gossip died down.

There was only one thing that the eldest young master didn't understand. How did those fake Boxers last night know that his brother was missing? Where could they have got the news? Did that mean that someone in the household or one of the shops was in league with them?

However, it was pointless to think about these things at present. Right now, the most important thing was to find his younger brother. If he was in trouble, the longer this all dragged out, the worse it would be for him.

CHAPTER 11

Illustration of a group of people in front of the French Consulate, 1900

THE MORE OUYANG ZUN thought about it, the more convinced he became that his younger brother was somewhere in the Foreign Concession. He was sure that he couldn't be wrong.

He had decided that there were only two possible explanations for his younger brother's disappearance: one was because of other people, the other was because of himself. If he had disappeared because of other people, that meant he'd been kidnapped. What would be the point of kidnapping him? It would be to extort money from his family. If this was what had occurred, then after such a long time had passed, someone ought to have contacted them with their demands. But weeks had gone by, and nothing had happened. The only approach made to them had come from that gang pretending to be Boxers. But this had only served to raise another question in his mind: who had told the fake Boxers that his younger brother was missing?

No matter what that was all about, it was impossible that Ouyang Jue had been kidnapped.

The other possible explanation lay with his younger brother himself. He had decided to run away – he'd gone to find that French woman. He seemed bewitched by her; that was for certain. Even though Mr Ma had explained that he was risking his life, he wasn't prepared to give her up; apparently, he didn't care if they killed him. It didn't matter whether he understood his brother's feelings or not – what mattered was that this was the real reason for his disappearance: he'd gone to the Foreign Concession.

He was quite convinced that his brother had vanished because he'd gone to join that foreign woman.

Ouyang Zun was a businessman through and through. He had a good head on his shoulders, and no matter how chaotic things got, he never lost his cool.

If he'd gone running over to the Foreign Concession, there could only be two possible results: either he'd been arrested by the Westerners, or he'd eloped with the French woman. But if they'd run off together, where could they possibly go? If he'd been arrested, they might well have shot him out of hand...

With that prospect in mind, the eldest young master was in a terrible state. But if he wanted to find out what had really happened, he would need to talk to Mr Ma. However, the fighting had already begun, and the old city and the Foreign Concession were at daggers drawn. How could he possibly get over there to ask his questions? He racked his brains to think of a way, and without letting his father know what he was doing, he set aside a really large amount of silver – for the first time in his life he raided the till at the paper shop. But whatever he tried, none of it worked. The situation was impossible – he spent an awful lot of money, but to no avail.

Ouyang Zun hadn't clapped eyes on Mr Ma since he last saw him over on Guyi Street. That time he'd risked his life to come over: he'd had to dress up in disguise, wearing smoked glasses and a false beard – he was really a good friend. After he'd slammed the door and stalked off, what had happened between the second young master and Mr Ma? How had he reacted? If his younger brother was obsessed with this woman, was it not possible that he'd forced Mr Ma to take him back out to the Foreign Concession again? He couldn't be sure; after all, he wasn't there, and guessing was no good.

Ouyang Zun knew an awful lot more about what was going on in the Foreign Concession than Ouyang Jue did. Some of his business involved the concession; although he didn't go there often, he did have to visit the place from time to time. He knew a number of people in the British and French Concessions. As for Chinese people who worked for Western companies, his acquaintance was not limited to Mr Ma – there was also a certain Second Master Xu, a native of Hangzhou. He was even more reliable than Mr Ma, and what is more, he had really good connections. Mr Ma could speak French, but Second Master Xu could also read and write. In the concession, he was regarded almost as a Westerner himself. He and Mr Ma both worked for foreign-owned firms, and his family was safely tucked away inside Zizhulin.

Mr Ma had many friends over in Tianjin proper. Ouyang Zun decided that he would begin by finding someone who could put him in touch with Mr Ma, but every lead he followed up ended in failure. Maybe he would get better results by asking a favour of Second Master Xu who knew so many people throughout the concession? Second Master Xu was a pretty popular guy. But when he considered this idea further, he decided it wouldn't work. Second Master Xu didn't know a thing about it, so he couldn't just send someone with a message – he risked having everyone gossiping about it! That was when he decided he would have to risk going to the concession himself. He spread some money around the local magistrate's office and the Maritime Customs' yamen, but the Qing artillery was fully occupied in shelling the foreigners, and the magistrate couldn't guarantee anything. Then, a well-informed friend told him that the new postal routes that had been set up in recent years remained in operation; mail vans were still running back and forth between the two sides. Businessmen leap on every opportunity they see, so Ouyang Zun immediately took advantage of this information. He bribed one of the assistant directors at the sorting office, and the next thing he knew he was bundled into a mail van. Luckily, this particular van was going in the right direction – the Great Qing Post Office. This beautiful grey-brick building was located right in the middle of the French Concession. If he could make it as far as the Great Qing Post Office, from there he could get to anywhere in the concession.

Once the mail van had made its way through the huge, rammed-earth Daying Gate, guarded by the Qing Army, it turned out onto the broad avenue running between the old city and the Foreign Concession. At this moment, he was looking at a battlefield – it was all quite different from how it normally appeared. On either side of a vast expanse of overgrown wasteland, he caught occasional glimpses of new entrenchments being constructed, military units being drilled or marching to and fro, and artillery pieces being manoeuvred into place. Out on this vast, unobstructed plain, you could clearly hear the roar of cannon fire from the north of the White River. Far in the distance, a gun would fire, and a long thin plume of smoke would streak across the blue sky. Occasionally, they came across craters in the road. There were foreigners out there supervising Chinese coolies as they repaired the damage. This road would be crucial when the colonial powers launched their attack against the old city of Tianjin.

As he expected, nobody tried to stop the van. After entering the concession and having passed through various temporary roadblocks set up by the foreigners, he discovered that the situation there seemed to be calm, but there were very few people to be seen.

Ouyang Zun got off the mail van and collected his thoughts. He knew his way around the French Concession perfectly well and had no difficulty in locating Mr Ma's residence. But the door was locked, and no matter how hard he knocked nobody came to open it. He was so desperate that he started to shout Mr Ma's name.

The door still didn't open. Instead, two French policemen walking their beat came over and started questioning him. The handful of French phrases he knew came in handy at this point. Although he couldn't even begin to explain what he was doing there, at least the two French policemen didn't see him as an enemy, so they let him go.

There was now nothing for it: he had to ask Second Master Xu for help.

Second Master Xu lived in a three-storey house topped with a domed roof over by the White River; this building was also his business premises. Two years earlier, he'd first made the acquaintance of Second Master Xu in that very house. He could remember pretty much where it was, so without too much effort he found his way there. When he knocked on the door, it transpired that Second Master Xu was at home. It really seemed like the light at the end of the tunnel.

Ouyang Zun had always been very fond of Second Master Xu – he was so straightforward and easy to deal with. He was friendly-looking, with fine skin, a round face with little eyes and a small nose set in it, and a thin straggly moustache. His hands were the size of hams, and so were his feet. A pot belly stuck out under his robe as if he'd stuffed a wok down there. Natives of Tianjin seldom looked anything like this. When he saw Ouyang Zun, he was so amazed that his mouth popped open and stayed that way for ages. Then he squawked, "Good Heavens, it's the eldest young master! What on earth are you doing here? Did they shoot you in from a cannon or what?" He smiled and invited Ouyang Zun into his house.

Ouyang Zun said, "I came in with the post office van."

"What a thing to think of doing! Right now, those vans are the only way of getting from one side to the other. I'm sure that means there's some emergency…"

"I'm looking for Mr Ma. I've just been to his house, but he's not at home," Ouyang Zun said. He only mentioned that he was looking for Mr Ma but didn't explain why. He was a businessman, after all, and businessmen always keep quiet about their true intentions. Until he had a good handle on what was going on, he wasn't going to say anything about what he was really doing here.

"I haven't seen him in ages. But he must be somewhere inside the concession – there's nowhere else he can go. He's a Christian, so the safest place for him right now is hiding somewhere around here," Second Master Xu said.

"If he's not at home, where else could he be?" Ouyang Zun enquired.

Second Master Xu smiled. "More than likely he's over in the church," he said. "There are lots of Christians hiding there, along with plenty of foreigners. The church is being guarded by the army, and it's a nice solid building. It'll be so much safer there than staying at home."

"There's more than one church in the French Concession! Which church will Mr Ma be hiding in?" Ouyang Zun asked.

"Of course he'll be in the Zizhulin church – the Church of St Louis. Right now, the Gordon Hall is the safest place in the British Concession, and the Church of St Louis is the safest place in the French Concession. It's the oldest church here, built around the same time as Notre-Dame des Victoires, and it's bigger and much more solidly built than the Drum Tower over in your part of town," Second Master Xu said. "It's not far from here – just three blocks away. I'll go with you." Second Master Xu was a very straightforward and warm-hearted man, so he was always happy to help.

"That would be wonderful! I can't speak French, so I can't just ask around," Ouyang Zun said quickly. At a time like this, finding someone willing to help can almost be a life-saving experience.

The two men emerged and turned to walk along the river. This gave Ouyang Zun a shock: the river was full of warships, and soldiers were massed on their decks with guns on their backs. They were all in uniform and lined up in orderly rows, wearing wide-brimmed flat hats and carrying duffel bags. The warships were bristling with huge cannons, pointing towards the northwest; apparently, they were all aimed at the old city. Countless brightly-coloured flags were fluttering in the wind coming off the river. Vast quantities of military equipment, not to mention cases of food, tents and horses, were being brought ashore from these ships.

The whole scene was very impressive. In its own way, it was as spectacular as the red lanterns he'd seen out on the Grand Canal the other day. It really looked like they were preparing for a great battle.

"Recently, many countries have been moving their troops here," Second Master Xu said. "We'd better leave. We don't want them to think that we are spies looking to gather military intelligence."

They moved away from the river as quickly as they could and turned down a cross street. The scene there was another shock for Ouyang Zun. Through the gaps in a wrought-iron fence, he could see a very large yard and a solidly-constructed, beautiful building with a row of tall stone pillars in front of it. A group of people were lined up in two rows. The front row were seated on chairs and stools, while the back row were all standing. Lots of them were armed with rifles; Ouyang Zun didn't know what on earth they were doing. He was afraid they might think he was a spy, so he speeded up. Then he suddenly realised that there were a couple of foreign women sitting in the front row. One of them was wearing a wide-brimmed straw hat and a long flowing skirt – she looked a little like Xénia.

In that moment of hesitation, Second Master Xu suddenly called out across the wrought-iron fence to the people over in the courtyard, then he turned to Ouyang Zun and said, "This is the French Consulate. I guess they're afraid that when fighting breaks out, they're going to find themselves scattered to the four winds. They're having a commemorative photograph done." Then he added, "A lot of them know me." All this time, he was waving and saying hello to his friends among the foreigners in the courtyard.

Ouyang Zun had now looked closely enough to discover that the foreign woman in the long skirt was middle-aged; it could not be Xénia. He followed Second Master Xu as he moved away. "They aren't soldiers, so why do they all have guns?" he asked Second Master Xu.

"All the foreigners in the concession are going around armed now," Second Master Xu informed him. "They are afraid the Boxers will attack. Oh yes, they are very frightened... very frightened indeed." The tones in which Second Master Xu spoke were enough to show the seriousness of the situation.

Although on the surface, the concession seemed calm, there was a terrible, invisible tension humming through the air.

After walking another block, they arrived at the Church of St Louis. Ouyang Zun felt sure that any moment now he would see his brother again.

The Church of St Louis had a real air of sanctity. This peculiar-looking church was built of Chinese bricks and stones – imposing and majestic. The pair of towers placed symmetrically on either side added to the impressive façade, while a series of long, narrow windows gave it a secretive, mysterious appearance. Perhaps because it was located so close to the White River and its miasmas, although the building was barely thirty years old, it was already mottled and stained with damp. On the north-facing wall, there were large patches of white efflorescence on the surface of the black bricks. Given that this was the oldest church in the Foreign Concession, it had always been the place of worship of choice for anyone of wealth and status; now it was their most precious place of sanctuary.

The guards at the main gate were heavily-armed soldiers. Ordinary people were not allowed inside. Since he could speak French quite fluently, Second Master Xu said a few words to the guards, and they sent someone in to have a look for them. Ouyang Zun still wasn't sure that Mr Ma was actually hiding there. After waiting for ages, he had pretty much decided that he wasn't to be found there. But just at that moment, Mr Ma came running out of the church.

Second Master Xu was always sensitive to atmosphere and quick to take his cues. He knew perfectly well that if Ouyang Zun was looking for Mr Ma at a moment like this, it must be because of some extraordinary crisis. Now that he had helped Ouyang Zun to find Mr Ma, he immediately made his excuses and left.

Ouyang Zun was absolutely desperate. He grabbed Mr Ma like a drowning man clutching at straws. Before Mr Ma had even had time to greet him, he demanded, "Where is my brother?" It seemed as though he expected Mr Ma to produce him immediately like a rabbit out of a hat.

"What?" Mr Ma exclaimed. "Is the second young master missing? When did that happen?"

"It's been more than two weeks. I haven't seen him since that day at Guyi Street when I walked out, slamming the door."

"How can that be?"

"It's true, I tell you, I haven't seen him since! He's disappeared!" the eldest young master said. He was horrified to discover that Mr Ma didn't know where his brother was, and now he was feeling even more desperate.

"Do you suspect me of being involved in some way? I risked my life that day to tell him not to come back to the concession."

"Of course I know you would not have brought him out here. But the fact remains that he just disappeared, and no one has seen him since that day. We've had no news of him for more than two weeks!"

What Mr Ma said next was an even bigger surprise for Ouyang Zun.

"That really is most odd. You know, Mademoiselle Xénia's disappeared too!"

"What?" Ouyang Zun didn't even notice he was shouting.

"You know who I'm talking about. Mademoiselle Xénia – the foreign woman your brother has been having an affair with – has disappeared... she's gone missing!"

"That's unbelievable!" Ouyang Zun could not imagine what could possibly have happened. He was no longer sure whether he was standing on his head or his heels. In his amazement, he started questioning himself. "Can they really have run off together?"

"There's no point in worrying about that. At a time like this, if he ran off with a foreign woman, where could he possibly go? For hundreds of miles around, the whole place is crawling with Boxers!"

"When did the foreign woman go missing?"

"I'm not sure exactly which day. Her father – he's an officer in the French Army – came to ask me if I'd seen her. He's in a terrible state of worry, but he's also angry. He's terrified that his daughter might have been kidnapped by the Boxers, and he's been looking everywhere for her."

"Does he know about the affair between my brother and his daughter?"

"No. There are only two people over here in the concession who saw Mademoiselle Xénia going off every day to that little white house to meet a young Chinese man. But they don't know who the Chinese man is, let alone that he has anything to do with me. Only you and I can know that."

"In your opinion, if the two of them have both gone missing, does that mean they've gone off together?" Ouyang Zun asked despairingly.

Today at this meeting, each of them had given the other a terrible message: something that the other could never have expected, something shocking and inconceivable. Ouyang Zun had told Mr Ma that his younger brother was missing, and Mr Ma had told Ouyang Zun that Xénia had gone too. If they had not disappeared together, why had they vanished at the same time? But if they had disappeared together, if they'd eloped with one another, where could they possibly have gone? To the Ouyang family's hometown of Cixi, outside Ningbo? Had they fled overseas to France? Could they have run away together without any real plan for where they were going, only to end up falling into the hands of the Boxers? No matter what theories Ouyang Zun came up with, the crucial thing was to find a way to determine what had actually happened. If he couldn't even do that, how was he ever going to find his brother?

Mr Ma knew two things that Ouyang Zun did not. One was that on the day they met at Guyi Street after Ouyang Zun slammed the door and walked away, Ouyang Jue had asked him to take a message to Xénia when he went back to the concession. He asked her to wait for him at that deserted and tumbledown white building. "I have to see her even if they kill me for it," he'd said. After his return to the Foreign Concession, Mr Ma hadn't said a word to Xénia. He was afraid of causing more trouble; he couldn't afford to annoy either the eldest young master, Ouyang Zun, or the French Army officer. The other thing he was keeping quiet about was that two days later, Xénia had suddenly appeared at his house and asked Mr Ma to go over to the old city to find Ouyang Jue, to tell him to meet her at the white building. She would be waiting there for him every day. She couldn't live without him.

Her tragic air, coupled with the way she seemed prepared to risk everything for love, moved Mr Ma. He was prepared to run the risk of going back to the old city again, but thinking it over, he decided he could not afford to anger either family. He didn't agree to help the unhappy, blue-eyed girl.

However, Mr Ma couldn't understand it: that day, Ouyang Jue had vowed that he would go to see Xénia that same day at the little white building over by the concession – he'd said he was determined to go even if they killed him. But had he actually gone? If he'd gone, why hadn't Xénia seen him? She was still waiting. It was all very odd.

Mr Ma had intended to tell Ouyang Zun about both these things, but he was afraid to speak lest Ouyang Zun think he'd become too closely involved in all of this. He'd already been dragged into too much of what had happened; he couldn't afford any further entanglements. On the one hand, he hoped to continue to do business with the Ouyang family in the future. On the other hand, if he told the foreign officer about the affair, that would be a total disaster for everyone. Now, with the two of them gone, this had turned into a missing-persons case. It was very unclear what could have happened to them. He really didn't want to get involved. He decided not to say anything and stay out of the matter. So he answered Ouyang Zun's question. "It's hard to say. Maybe, maybe not. But they are the only ones who can tell you – what do we know?" He added some words of vain regret. "I blame myself for passing on Mademoiselle Xénia's invitation for the second young master to visit her in the Foreign Concession – otherwise, none of this would have happened." Then he added, "I simply can't understand – they don't have a language in common, so they can't talk to each other. Neither of them can understand what the other one is saying. How can this have happened? They've got so they don't care if they get themselves killed."

Mr Ma was puzzled. He shook his head and sighed.

Ouyang Zun waved him away. "Don't say any more, there's no point," he said. "Since he's not here, I'd better get back to the old city. The postal van will be waiting for me."

Mr Ma escorted him as far as the Great Qing Post Office on Central Avenue. He was just in time. A large number of soldiers from the Eight-Nation Alliance had just disembarked and were now lining up on the main roads running through the middle of the concession. Afterwards, they were going to march towards the Gordon Hall in the British Concession. Having hastily said goodbye to Mr Ma, he clambered aboard the mail van. As soon as it crossed the road, it was closed. A group of foreign soldiers marched south, stepping in unison to the beat of a drum. The forceful sound of their leather boots stamping on the ground was very frightening; all of those thousands of shiny black guns formed a murderous thicket. His ears were assaulted by constant drumrolls and bugle calls. He couldn't help saying to the driver, "Come on! Let's get out of here quick! Hurry!" He couldn't wait for the postal van to leave.

On his way back to the old city in the van, Ouyang Zun suddenly started to cry. The assistant director at the postal sorting office who'd gone with him couldn't understand what was wrong. When he asked, Ouyang Zun didn't reply. He'd gone out to the Foreign Concession full of hope that he'd be able to find his younger brother. He was quite sure he was there. If he was in the hands of one of the foreign powers, he was determined to find a way to bring him back safe and sound. He had not been expecting that not only would he fail to find his brother, but he'd also be told that the French woman had disappeared too.

Things were getting more and more complicated.

Ouyang Zun felt as if he were on a boat that had finally reached its longed-for harbour after a thousand travails. Just as he came in sight of land, the harbour had sunk into the depths of a vast ocean stretching as far as the eye could see.

His last hope was gone.

His brother had gone. He'd disappeared, and nobody knew whether he was dead or alive. He cried, and when he put his hands up to cover his face, the tears came trickling out between his fingers.

After getting off the mail van and making his way back to the walled city, Ouyang Zun realised that the whole place felt quite different. There were altars set up on both sides of the main roads, and in front of every house you could see red lanterns wreathed by wisps of incense smoke. The smell of burning incense hung so thick in the air it seemed as if the whole city were nothing but a giant temple. Ouyang Zun was feeling so upset that he didn't really notice any of this. He didn't ask what was going on: he didn't care.

When he arrived home, by the entrance to the house he saw a basket of 'Victory' cakes and a tureen of sweet mung-bean soup. The red lacquer altar that they normally used for the City God's festival was there too, with an incense burner placed on top of it. According to the customs of the Militia of Righteous Harmony, the offerings consisted of a bowl of water and three plain steamed buns. Zhang Yi was there keeping an eye on things, a red turban wrapped around his head. When they met, he told the eldest young master that the Boxers had just fought an engagement with the foreign devils at Majiakou, and the devils had run off with their tails between their legs. He acted out for him how Master Cao of the Kan Division and Master Zhang of 'Number One Division' had gone to the front line in person to cast spells on their troops, and how the Boxers had then flown over to the Foreign Concession, scattering smouldering incense down from the skies to set fire to the buildings there, burning countless numbers of them to the ground. Ouyang Zun had just come back from the concession, and he hadn't seen a single building there on fire. He knew this story was completely untrue, but he was hardly in a position to refute it, so he said nothing and just went in through the gate.

Every day when he got home, he would go and say hello to his father.

These days, every time he saw his father, to begin with he wouldn't say a word. It seemed that he was waiting for news – news about what had happened to Ouyang Jue. Every time he would shake his head in silence. Father would then point to a chair, and he would sit down. His father wouldn't ask any questions in order to avoid further disappointment.

Today, however, Father seemed to have something to say to him. First, he asked, "Do you see the situation improving?"

"I think that war will break out pretty soon," Ouyang Zun replied.

"Do you think our army and the Boxers can beat the foreigners?" his father asked.

"At least six or seven thousand foreign soldiers arrived in the concession today," Ouyang Zun told him. "Troops have even come from Russia and Italy."

"Those countries don't have concessions here," his father remarked. "They must be thinking that if they win this war, they'll be able to demand concessions of their own." Old Master Ouyang had a very keen grasp of the current political situation.

"True," Ouyang Zun said. "Japan has also sent a lot of soldiers. At present, the White River is chock-a-block with foreign warships, and they are bringing up a lot of modern artillery pieces."

"How do you know that? You can't have gone to the Foreign Concession to see for yourself…" Old Master Ouyang asked curiously.

He realised he'd spoken out of turn, and quickly covered up his mistake. "I happened to bump into one of the assistant directors at the post office, and he told me about it. They are still going back and forth, sending mail and taking it out. Although diplomatic relations have officially been broken off, there are still some government documents that need to be transmitted, and they are going by post."

Old Master Ouyang pondered this information for a moment. Then he sighed and said, "It will be hard for one country to defeat eight. The colonial powers are all hand-in-glove together, but our government and the Militia of Righteous Harmony are just allied on the surface – deep down there are plenty of divisions."

"You are quite right," Ouyang Zun said. "General Nie of the Front Division of the Wuwei Army has been trying to put down the Boxer Rebellion all this time. Apparently, even now there is still fighting going on between his men and the Militia."

It was now time for his father to say what he actually wanted to tell him. "I think you and Xifeng ought to go back to our old hometown in Ningbo to get away from all of this. We've still got our house back there, and the caretakers have been looking after it."

Ouyang Zun was stunned. "How could I possibly do that?" he demanded. "What about you? If anybody is going to go back, it should be you. I couldn't possibly abandon you here like this! I can keep an eye on things here."

"I'm not going anywhere. I'm staying right here. There is no need for you to worry about our paper shops. Once war breaks out they'll both go up in flames – there's nothing anyone can do to stop it. The last two days, I've packed up all the valuables in the house – I want you to take them with you. Tomorrow you're to go to both of the paper shops and make sure everything is in order. Make sure you remove anything important or valuable. In particular, I need you to pack up all the account books and bring them back here. You've got to leave within the next three days because if you delay any longer than that, you won't be able to get away. There are plenty of families that have already left." Old Master Ouyang seemed sombre, but his orders were clear. Everything had been arranged, and he was just tying up a few loose ends.

Ouyang Zun was a little worried. "Why won't you go back home to wait this out?"

"I'm waiting for your brother," he said calmly.

"I can do that better than you – after all, I can go out and look for him," Ouyang Zun said.

"I don't think you're going to find him no matter how hard you look. We'll just have to wait," Old Master Ouyang replied.

Ouyang Zun hadn't realised his father had thought the whole thing out so clearly. "There's another reason that I can't go," his father continued, "and that's Shuxian. She doesn't say a word all day. She doesn't look in the least worried. But you know… she spends all day every day sitting in her room peeling melon seeds for your brother. She's already got three massive jars full. She's not right in the head any more, and she's sure to refuse to go... I can't possibly just leave her here all by herself! As long as I'm here, she'll try and keep herself pulled together. If I leave, it will kill her." He paused for a moment, and his face suddenly became very dignified. He then said decidedly, "I will not leave under any circumstances!"

Old Master Ouyang spoke like a warrior swearing that he would die rather than surrender.

This made Ouyang Zun extremely sad. Overwhelmed by his emotions, his legs buckled, and he fell to his knees in front of his father.

CHAPTER 12

Young Boxers photographed during martial arts practice

For many days, Ouyang Jue worked away under Zhu San's supervision, and he kept to the rules he'd set down for himself: don't listen, don't hear, don't look and don't ask. Every morning, he would go from the stable to the warehouse where he would be keeping the accounts up to date; then in the evening, he went back to the stable to sleep. Walking back and forth across the courtyard, he never so much as glanced to left or right; he just kept moving, his head bowed. All he could see were the shadows cast by the men posted on the roofs. In the morning, it was the shadows of the Militia members on guard on the roof of the east wing that fell across the courtyard, slanting westwards; in the evening, it was the shadows of the Militia members on the roof of the west wing that fell across the courtyard, leaning eastwards. He didn't see anything else. He was terrified that one day Third Brother might suddenly turn on him and say, "No one is prepared to vouch for you. You must be a spy. Take this man out and cut his head off!"

This fear tormented him every day.

One evening, when they had finished work at the warehouse, Zhu San handed him over to a Militia member who escorted him back to the stable. When he entered the smelly dark room, he saw that he'd been joined by two more people: a man and a woman were sitting up against the wall. "You are not allowed to talk," the Militia member said sternly. Then he closed the door and walked away.

As soon as the door was closed, it became pitch-dark inside the stable. In the confused moment just as he came through the door, he saw that both these people had their hair loose – the woman had her hair down, and the man had his queue undone. They both appeared very dishevelled, but beyond that he hadn't been able to see what they looked like at all.

They did not dare to speak.

Before the sun set, there would still be a lot of racket outside. Later, there was less and less noise as gradually they quietened down. Inside the room, it seemed even quieter and even darker. Of the two of them, it was the man who spoke first. "How many days have you been here? Why did they arrest you?" His voice was very low and very small, but he could hear it perfectly clearly.

"For a while." He did not dare say more.

"Will they cut your head off?"

"They haven't done it yet." He said that because it was meaningless.

"Oh, sure. Are you a Christian?"

"Are you?" He didn't answer the question; he just turned it around.

"Yes indeed! All the Christians near us have run away. Although not all of them have had their heads cut off, if you've got enemies locally, they could easily get you killed. We're from Nanpi. Where are you from?"

"Nanpi is so far away. How did you end up being brought here?" He kept on asking questions since he didn't want to answer any. He already knew how to survive here.

"We came here to try and hide in the Foreign Concession. We were almost there when we got caught. I guess we were unlucky," the man said.

Ouyang Jue didn't respond. He had made up his mind that he would never take the initiative to speak. If the man asked him a question, he would say as little as possible.

There was silence for a moment. Then the woman whispered something to the man, but he couldn't hear what she said.

Suddenly, the man said angrily to the woman, "It's no use blaming me. It's our fate that's brought us here, and if they kill us, they kill us! Everyone dies sooner or later, don't they? There's nothing to be afraid of."

"But I am afraid," the woman cried.

"If feeling frightened means you do something to get out of here, then go right ahead. If it doesn't help, there's no point in being afraid. If you're afraid in that kind of situation, you're just scaring yourself."

The woman kept on crying, so they stopped talking.

Ouyang Jue had been working hard all day, so he now fell into a confused sleep. At some point, the door opened with a bang. Several Militia members came in holding flaming torches and broadswords, shouting, "Stand up! Stand up right now!"

The two people from Nanpi stood up. Ouyang Jue thought that

this had nothing to do with him and just sat still. A Militia member called out to him, "You too. Let's go!"

Ouyang Jue's legs almost gave way beneath him. Even though he managed to get to his feet, he could not move. He could never have imagined that it would be so easy to die. It could happen in the blink of an eye.

When the Boxers took them out into the courtyard, the sky was growing light. You couldn't see anything clearly, but the shadows were sharp. The Boxers escorted them out through the back of the courtyard and across a patch of woodland, skirting a small pond and then up to the top of a hill. Dense clumps of reeds at the foot of the hill indicated that there might be further ponds below. One of the Boxers told them to kneel down facing the reeds. Ouyang Jue was quite sure that his last moments had come. Everything went black before his eyes, and his body crumpled. He would have pitched head first down the slope if he had not been caught and held by the Boxer standing right behind him.

A Boxer rested his gleaming sword right on the necks of the two people from Nanpi and asked in a sharp voice, "Have you been using your position to bully other people? If you dare lie, we'll behead you here and now!"

People facing the prospect of their imminent demise are different from how they are in their day-to-day lives. The woman who had been so afraid of death turned out to be pretty tough, saying loudly, "No!" The man who had appeared quite unafraid now couldn't say a word – clearly, he'd done things he wasn't prepared to talk about.

Suddenly, a loud voice came from behind them. "Kill them!"

The Boxer raised his sword, and then it fell – in an instant, two heads rolled down the hill towards the reed beds. The reeds were so dense that there was a brief rustling, and then the heads disappeared from view.

The Boxer put the icy blade of his broadsword against Ouyang Jue's neck and asked sharply, "Are you a spy? If you dare to lie, we'll behead you right now!"

At that moment, Ouyang Jue no longer felt afraid. If he was going to die, it didn't matter what he said. He opened his mouth and spoke the truth. "My family runs a paper shop. I haven't done anything wrong. I'm not a Christian either."

After a long pause, the same loud voice came from behind him. "Take him back!"

What? They weren't going to cut his head off? Was he going to live? He couldn't believe it. What on earth was going on? On the way back to the village, his legs were still as soft as noodles, so he was dragged along by two Militia members. All of a sudden, he realised that the person walking in front of him had a familiar back – Third Brother!

So it was Third Brother who had saved his life!

When he got back to the warehouse, Zhu San was casting his accounts as usual. On seeing him, he said lightly, "There you are." He indicated a stool and asked him to sit down.

Ouyang Jue just sat on that stool for a long time, recovering from his shock.

"After today, you don't need to go back to the stable any more," Zhu San told him. "You can stay with me in the courtyard out front." Then he got up and tossed him a bag of clothes, saying, "Third Brother wants you to wear these in future."

He opened it up and saw that there were some old clothes inside, together with a wide strip of blue cloth. This was the kind of sash that the Boxers wore.

He felt stunned. For many days now, he'd been the victim of continuous bad luck, so he could no longer tell whether all the things that had happened to him that day were good or bad. How could this be? Two days later, Ouyang Jue finally worked out what had happened and its implications. It seemed that all this time he'd been under secret observation; they'd been watching everything he said and did. Had they been to the old city to ask around? He didn't know and didn't dare to ask. However, they obviously didn't think he was a spy. The clothes that Third Brother had given him to wear, particularly the blue sash that was the symbol of the Militia of Righteous Harmony, demonstrated that they were now prepared to trust him.

In addition, Third Brother was allowing him to move out of the stable, which meant that he was no longer being regarded as a prisoner. The reason he would now be living with Zhu San might be that the latter couldn't do without him, or it might be that Third Brother wanted Zhu San to continue to keep an eye on him – it was hard to say. In recent days, he'd been working with Zhu San and had put a lot of effort into buttering him up. Everyone else just called him Zhu San, but he addressed him as Third Master Zhu; that was the custom of people in the old city of Tianjin – 'Master' was a standard term of respect. Zhu San absolutely loved it. Although he was literate and numerate, nobody in his village had ever had any particular respect for him. Now, an educated young man from the big city was calling him 'Third Master Zhu' day in and day out, so of course he felt good – it gave him face. When Ouyang Jue was writing out his accounts, he deliberately wrote the words awkwardly, making them crooked and ugly, so as not to make Zhu San jealous. It seemed that he was getting better at dealing with people.

So had Zhu San, a man whose nose hair came curling out of his nostrils, put in a good word for him with Third Brother?

Sometimes you will never know why your luck has changed.

The courtyard in which Ouyang Jue had now moved into was very much the same as the one in which he'd been living up until now. There were three or four trees there, and a well in the middle. This was a residential courtyard, with seven or eight rooms. Even though there weren't many rooms, there were an awful lot of people living there. These people did all kinds of jobs around the shrine. There were drummers, trumpeters, executioners, grooms for the horses, cooks and so on, while he and Zhu San were the accountants. All of them took orders from Third Brother. They were busy at their own tasks every day, rushing back and forth. That meant that security here was a little less tight, and people were allowed to chat – even gossip a bit, but many topics remained off-limits. By contrast, the other courtyard was really strictly guarded, and not even a dog or cat could sneak in or out. In order to get through the door, you had to have the password, and it changed every day; today it was "Total Victory", and then tomorrow it would be "White Horse". Zhu San told him what the password was every day.

Third Brother came past from time to time; there seemed to be no regular pattern. Every time he turned up, it was because he had some task to perform there. If he didn't need them for anything, he wouldn't bother. Third Brother was quick and decisive; everything he did, even drinking water or just walking along, he did at high speed. He never wasted words, and he never gossiped with anyone. His eye was keen and his manner aggressive. Anyone who had to speak to him wouldn't dare to look him in the face. If the Militia of Righteous Harmony's base at the Gao Family Village could be compared to a cart, then Third Brother was the axle. Every other part of the cart relied on him and rotated around him. Although the situation seemed so complicated and hard to understand, he apparently felt under no pressure. He seemed capable of dealing with whatever came up, and nothing seemed to faze him – it was as if he could do absolutely anything he put his mind to.

Having moved out of that dark, smelly, stuffy and hot stable, Ouyang Jue felt so much better; he could even breathe more easily. After dinner, he could now go with Zhu San and sit out in the courtyard under one of the trees, enjoying the breeze, or take a bucket of cold well-water to wash the sweat off his body.

A large area of flat land was situated opposite the courtyard. This was the Gao Family Village's facility for drying and milling rice. The ground there was hard and impacted, having been rolled year after year by the heavy stone rollers used for removing the husks from rice. Now there were various stone blocks and weights there, together with heavy swords. These were used by Militia members when they were practising martial arts. There was a large house up on the bluff overlooking this ground to the north. People said that the granary down here belonged to a family that had lived over in that house, but now, the Militia was using the place as their headquarters. From that distance, he could see that there were two big poles erected by the gate, each with a golden-yellow flag fluttering from the top, embroidered with large red characters. The left-hand side read, "The Militia of Righteous Harmony is on the Right Path." On the right, it said, "Assist the Qing to Expel All Westerners." There was another pole in the middle, from which was suspended a square flag with a single black character – "Liu" – embroidered on a red background. This one enormous word was fully a yard across. Banners and weapon racks were arranged in an impressive array, spreading out on either side. The brightly-coloured ribbons and tassels trimming the banners danced in the wind; meanwhile, the swords, spears and halberds in the weapon racks shone with a silver gleam. Below, there was a sutra table with its ends curled up, with a large antique incense burner on top. This must have been taken from some temple. Incense was burned in that brazier all day, wreathing it in pale smoke. Strangely, no one was standing guard outside – in fact, the whole place seemed empty and bare. There was often a flock of birds hopping about here and there. It was bizarrely quiet, as if there might be some god or spirit in residence in the house.

Was Liu Nineteen living there? No one asked. In fact, no one dared to ask.

The finest spectacle offered by the Militia headquarters was the roll call held every morning and evening at the milling ground.

During the roll call, all the people and horses attached to the Militia headquarters had to line up in order at the ground, including Zhu San. Ouyang Jue was the only person not required to attend because he was not a member of the Militia of Righteous Harmony; his name was not included on their lists. The most eye-catching units in the entire division were Liu Nineteen's mobile artillery, with four hundred people in each battalion and three battalions in total, numbering twelve thousand men in all. The Militia didn't have a uniform, so they were all wearing their usual clothes, but their turbans and sashes were blue. The mobile artillery battalions were different; they all wore dark blue shirts and blue trousers, but their turbans and sashes were black. Their sleeves were tied back, they had puttees wound round their legs, and they carried guns on their backs. All of them seemed extraordinarily impressive. Even at first glance, they looked to be fantastically brave warriors. Apparently, all members of the mobile artillery battalions had mounts, but when the roll call was made, only the people were mustered, not the horses. As soon as the mobile artillery units arrived, it gave the morale of everyone at headquarters a boost. That was the reason it was necessary to hold a roll call twice a day, morning and evening.

Once all the Militia rank and file had lined up, the five Brothers would come walking out of their headquarters. These men were the generals under Liu Nineteen's command, and every time there was a roll call they were sure to be present. Up until this time, Ouyang Jue had only ever set eyes on Elder and Third Brother. The dark-skinned Elder Brother stood in the centre, and the other four Brothers lined up on either side of him, as if they were generals on a stage. Then the names of the members of the group were called out one by one from the roster. This process was strictly observed and took a long time. At the end of roll call, Third Brother would lead the entire company in chanting the words on the flags: "The Militia of Righteous Harmony is on the Right Path... Assist the Qing to Expel All Westerners."

About two or three thousand people took part each time in the roll call. There were so many people that they couldn't all fit within the confines of the rice-milling ground, so some of them would stand outside in any space they could find, along the roads or out among the trees. When they shouted in unison, the sound could be heard for miles around, an ear-splitting noise that shook the ground.

However, their leader, Master Liu Nineteen, never appeared. Ouyang Jue thought that the thin man he'd been imprisoned with in the stables in the beginning had it right: not even members of his own headquarters had the chance to meet Liu Nineteen face-to-face. He had to be living somewhere around here, but he didn't dare to ask – everyone knew that trying to find out about what Liu Nineteen was up to was completely taboo. You must be up to something. He'd heard that anyone asking questions about Liu Nineteen would have their tongue cut out.

Two weeks earlier, when Ouyang Jue's life was hanging in the balance, the only idea in his head was how to survive. Now that he knew he was going to live, his hopes for the future gradually revived. In the evening, to the sound of Zhu San's snoring, his father, eldest brother and Shuxian came into his mind. He missed them so much! They could have no idea of where he was or what had happened to him. They would be ignorant of all that had happened – they must be so worried, searching everywhere for him. Although Shuxian would be terribly worried, she would never just sit and cry all day. She was not that kind of woman. If you cut her arm with a knife, she would stay silent, hiding the wound in her sleeve. She wouldn't hate you for it, or hold a grudge, nor would she seek revenge; never, never, never!

He began to feel sorry for hurting such a fine woman…

But when he'd so lightly fallen in love with Xénia – how could he fail to be deeply moved by such an intelligent, beautiful, honest, and at the same time profoundly sexy foreign woman? On the one hand, there was the wife chosen for him by his father; on the other, there was this woman he'd found for himself. The moment she came into his mind, yet again she proved simply irresistible. Yet again, she took hold of him with her soft white hand and led him away; yet again, they were running through the deserted white building; yet again, he fulfilled his deepest fantasies. He began to remember with excitement how wildly he'd explored her most intimate places, how he'd burrowed head first under her skirt, how they'd pillowed against each other stark naked, how they'd both closed their eyes and drawn the outline of each other's body with kisses… All the crazy and romantic details of their past encounters could be vividly replayed in his mind once he was sure that the Boxers were not planning to separate his head from his shoulders with one sweep of the blade.

One day, he suddenly seemed to smell that special fragrance that made his heart beat faster. He had missed that scent. But when he tried to sense it again, he could not. Apparently, smell is impossible to call to mind at will. Often throughout this time, he felt that he reached for Xénia but could not take hold of her. She'd become ethereal and illusory. He was afraid that he would lose her.

Was she waiting for him over at that small white house?

For some reason, he was always totally convinced that she was still waiting for him. Although she'd never promised him that she would do so, he was sure she'd be there. Was this conviction born from the pure, deep expression in Xénia's eyes? That expression had more than once appeared in the deepest part of his heart. This kept alive the idea of escape, and he even began to think about how he might achieve this.

Ouyang Jue managed to steal a blue headcloth from the warehouse. He already had a blue sash. He planned to disguise himself as a member of the Militia and run away at some point when his captors were not paying attention.

Two days after Ouyang Jue stole the blue cloth, Zhu San was busy at his accounts, while he was sorting out various things behind him. All of a sudden, Zhu San said, "Do you want to join the Militia of Righteous Harmony?"

As soon as he heard this, he was so scared that he couldn't move. He thought that Zhu San had discovered that he'd stolen the headcloth and was going to try and escape. That alone was enough to take him to the block. Just as Ouyang Jue was about to kneel down and beg for mercy, Zhu San continued, "It's not easy to join the Militia. You'll have to wait for Third Brother to come and ask you. Do you know what questions Third Brother will ask?"

Ouyang Jue now realised that Zhu San hadn't noticed a thing; he was just chatting. He made haste to answer. "How should I know?" He looked obviously flustered, but luckily, he was standing behind Zhu San, who remained oblivious.

"He will ask you if you are afraid to die," Zhu San said. "The Militia doesn't want cowards."

Zhu San then buried his head in his accounts again.

Just as Ouyang Jue was worrying that he would never find a way to escape, Third Brother sent him and Zhu San to the west of the village.

Elder Brother had been fighting with the foreigners over at the Temple of Buddha's Light, and he'd captured some horses and guns. This loot was all piled up on the west side of the village. Elder Brother had plans to establish another mobile artillery unit in the vicinity, so it would be a waste of time to transport them back to the warehouse only to have to return them to where they'd come from in the first place. So Third Brother asked them to bring their brushes and account books over to the west of the village to make an inventory on the spot.

Ouyang Jue soon realised that the route that took them to the western edge of the village was very quiet. There were a few cottages off to the right, but on the left there was just an endless vista of shallow depressions, with no sign of human habitation anywhere. Moreover, the trees here grew very dense, offering all sorts of places to hide. As they walked on, they had to make their way through a forest of willow trees, whose long straggly branches hung down all the way to the ground. As they pushed past, they had to keep pulling the willow branches aside, just like parting a thick curtain. This would be a great way to make his escape.

As Ouyang Jue pulled aside the willow branches, far in the distance he saw a wide expanse of flat land. Beyond that lay a row of low cottages. To his surprise, there were large numbers of sentries standing guard all over the plain. The Militia posted there were all members of the black-clad mobile artillery battalions. Why did this place need to be so strictly guarded? All of a sudden, Zhu San, who was walking behind him, came up and gave him such a tug backwards it almost pulled him off his feet. In a low voice, he whispered to him, "We can't go any further. That's where Master Liu lives."

Liu Nineteen lived in this remote and horrible place! In spite of the fact that it was a very hot day, the chills gave him goosebumps all over.

Zhu San said nervously, "We've gone the wrong way – we should have turned west a while back. We shouldn't have come this far. If they spot us, they'll think we're spies."

"I was wondering why there were so many people on guard here…"

"What you see now are just the sentries that they have out in the open. There'll be more that you don't see. For ten miles in each direction, the place is crawling with hidden sentinels. Out of all the divisions of the Militia of Righteous Harmony, it's this place that's under the heaviest guard. And it's not just here to the west of the village – the whole of Gao Family Village is the same."

Zhu San spoke with great pride, but it was a terrible shock for Ouyang Jue. Every hope of being able to escape was extinguished then and there.

CHAPTER 13

German troops from the Eight-Nation Alliance advancing

WHEN ONE HOPE DIES, another springs into life in its place.

Since Gao Family Village was so tightly guarded that he could not possibly hope to escape, Ouyang Jue was forced to come up with another idea. He was now planning to run away while the Militia was off fighting with the Westerners.

The Militia of Righteous Harmony was there to launch an attack on the Foreign Concession, weren't they? If he went with them, he could waltz straight into Zizhulin – maybe even make his way to the little white house he'd seen so many times in his dreams. However, if this was what he wanted to do, he had to join the Militia of Righteous Harmony first. And if he wanted to join the Militia – well, as Zhu San had told him, he had to be unafraid to risk his life, and he had to know some martial arts.

He rushed off to the milling ground to practise lifting the stone weights there. The heaviest thing he'd ever lifted before was an inkstone, and that was nothing – nothing at all – compared with this. There was no point thinking about practising; he couldn't even pick up the lightest one. Each of the stone weights he tried to lift seemed to be rooted to the ground and wouldn't move no matter how hard he tugged at them.

Zhu San was standing on the slope watching him. With a smile, he said, "You're nothing but a bookworm! Twiddling about with a brush is as much as you can manage, so don't bother with these things. Come over here, and I'll teach you a trick or two."

"What are you going to teach me?" Ouyang Jue asked. He didn't believe that he had anything to learn from this peasant who could barely manage to scratch out a few wonky characters on a page.

Zhu San took him round to the back of the warehouse and fished out some square pieces of yellow joss paper on which he proceeded to draw some strange squiggles with a brush dipped first in black ink and then in red. These squiggles looked a bit like calligraphy but weren't; they also looked a bit like a painting, but they weren't that either.

"Is that some kind of talisman text?" Ouyang Jue asked.

"You've seen this kind of thing before?" Zhu San enquired.

"I have seen them in Daoist temples."

"Do you know what they are for?"

"To ask for divine assistance, to expel demons, to avoid misfortune, as protection..."

Zhu San then asked him, "Have you ever requested someone to make you a talisman? Did it work?"

"No." He smiled and added, "I've just heard people talking about it."

"This is the talisman that Master Liu gives his men," Zhu San explained. "Do you know its magic power?"

"What magic power?" he asked. He'd never heard of such a thing before.

Zhu San grinned but didn't answer. He heard a voice behind him – not loud, but very clear. "Let me explain."

He looked around and saw a man standing behind him. It was Third Brother.

After Third Brother had said hello to Zhu San, he asked him to go into the warehouse and find him a cutlass. The cutlass was very heavy. It was encased in a shagreen scabbard with a bronze mount. The hilt was ornamented with a big red tassel. Third Brother put his hand down on the hilt and drew the sword with a soft *swish* – the blade of the cutlass emerged like a dazzling silver crescent moon. The moment the blade came out from its scabbard, there was a sudden chill. Ouyang Jue could not help flinching.

Third Brother watched this with a slight curl of the lip. He asked Ouyang Jue to lift up his jacket. Ouyang Jue rucked up his jacket to expose his soft white stomach, not understanding in the least what this could possibly be for. Third Brother came right up to him, with the cutlass held at an angle. This scared Ouyang Jue so much that he took a step backwards.

Third Brother said, "Stand still! I'm not going to kill you. If I was going to kill you, I'd have done it long ago!" As he said this, he gently touched Ouyang Jue's stomach with the edge of the shining blade.

It was so quick that he didn't feel a thing; but there was now a bright red line across his stomach, and blood was dripping down from it. If Third Brother had used just a fraction more force, he would have been eviscerated. Before Ouyang Jue had even had time to scream, Third Brother had already put his weapon down. Next to him, Zhu San took a pinch of grey powder from a small bag and smeared it across Ouyang Jue's bleeding wound. Ouyang Jue knew that this was 'Dragon Bone' powder, which was used by the Militia as an anti-haemorrhagic when they were injured in battle.

Ouyang Jue had no idea why Third Brother had done this, but then he saw him hand the cutlass over to Zhu San as he removed his vest, leaving him naked from the waist up. When Third Brother was fully clothed, you would have no idea of how strong he was. Now that he'd taken his vest off, a shockingly hard body was revealed, with the muscles bulging beneath his skin. Third Brother picked up the talisman that Zhu San had just drawn, touched it with a little flour paste, and then *bam* – he'd slapped it against his stomach. Then he crossed his arms, closed his eyes and concentrated on moving the *qi* within his body. A few moments later, his belly bulged a little. He kept reciting the same weird incantation over and over again. "The Tripitaka Monk and the River Ogre Sha Wujing... The Eight Precepts Pig and the Enlightened Monkey." His stomach was now protruding even further and becoming hard.

Suddenly, Third Brother opened his eyes. His eyeballs had rolled round so far in his head that all you could see were the whites, and they shone with an aggressive light. He shouted to Zhu San, "Come on! Hit me now!"

Zhu San must have been out of his mind. He swung the cutlass in his hands and slashed it straight across Third Brother's stomach. Ouyang Jue was so horrified he screamed at the top of his voice; he thought Zhu San was actually going to kill Third Brother. However, the most amazing thing happened. It was as if the blade had hit a rock – there was a *clang* just like that, and even though the cutlass had definitely struck him, Third Brother's stomach was completely uninjured. There was just a white mark there, like what you see when you sharpen an axe against a whetstone.

After giving him this slash, Zhu San did not stop. It was followed by another. Yet again, Ouyang Jue screamed, but there was nothing but a white mark left behind. He hacked at him again and again, until there were a dozen or more white marks crisscrossing Third Brother's skin.

Suddenly, Zhu San stopped and threw the cutlass down on the

ground with a *clang*. He was panting, and beads of sweat pearled his forehead.

Third Brother behaved as if nothing in the least out of the ordinary had happened. He rubbed his stomach with his hands, and very soon it had flattened out and softened up again. The white marks across it had now turned into pale pink wheals. As he put his vest back on, he said to Ouyang Jue, "Once the spell has been cast, if you have that talisman on your sword, you can take foreign heads. If you put it on a Western building, it'll burn to the ground. And if you put it on yourself, no sword or gun can touch you!" Then he pointed to Zhu San and said, "He drew this talisman. If you take him as your master, he'll teach you how to draw them too!"

He would never have guessed that Zhu San had such amazing, magical abilities. Ouyang Jue, who was gaping open-mouthed at the sight with his eyes practically starting from his head, went down on his knees and called on "Third Master Zhu" to accept him as a disciple. Zhu San was grinning from ear to ear. Before this, when he'd called him "Third Master Zhu" it was just to try and butter him up, but now he was going to be teaching him, he really did qualify as a "Master".

If he learned how to draw talismans, did that make him a member of the Militia of Righteous Harmony? Would he have the opportunity to go with them when they attacked Zizhulin?

In the first week of June, the fighting seemed to suddenly take a turn for the worse. Although Ouyang Jue did not dare to make the slightest mistake in word or deed, he kept his eyes and ears open, watching the situation and waiting for his opportunity.

For the first two days, the gunfire was mostly over towards the Foreign Concession. Although it was a long way away, it could be heard quite clearly. This was a wilderness; the whole place was flat as a pancake with not a single hump as far as the eye could see, so even the chirruping of a bird could be heard for miles around. A few days ago, the gunfire was still mostly quite sporadic. It was only every so often that they kept up a barrage. But yesterday, the guns were firing without the slightest let-up for an hour or two at a time. When the cannon fire was so concentrated, it became all of a piece, like the rumbling of thunder when dark clouds roll across the sky.

Gazing off towards the horizon, far away to the north and northeast, you could just make out puffs of smoke. Under the noonday sun, these fluffy plumes seemed as insubstantial as wisps of cloud. In the twilight towards dusk, they became much thicker and inky-black, floating up into the sky like demons or devils.

It seemed that the war had now really begun, and the fighting was becoming more and more fierce. But it was impossible to tell which side was stronger, and who was going to win.

Today, the gunfire was even worse. Now it was not just the sound of the cannons going off – they could also hear rifles being fired with a sharp crack. Clearly, the battlefield could not be far away. This made everyone very nervous. Later on, Ouyang Jue heard that Liu Nineteen's men had been involved in a terrible fight – the worst since their arrival at the Gao Family Village. Because he had too many soldiers under his command, it was impossible to muster all of his men and their horses on the village's milling ground, so they'd had to run out to the wasteland to the southwest to go into battle formation. When his three battalions set off, they'd trampled the crops growing there flat into the muck. Fortunately, because of the drought, the rice crop had failed right from the beginning, and it had been left as straw. Once everyone had stamped all over it, they might as well have run a stone roller over the place – all of the desiccated seedlings were lying flat on the ground.

Elder Brother was in overall command of the troops. He even got to order Master Liu's own mobile artillery units into battle. Third Brother was left behind to guard Gao Family Village with his force of one thousand Militia members; they didn't want the foreigners attacking their base from behind.

Pretty much everyone who lived in the same courtyard as Ouyang Jue had gone. They'd all been sent to the front: the scouts, flag signalmen, drummers, buglers and so on. Even Zhu San had gone. Apparently, there were so many soldiers in the field that they didn't have enough talismans. When Elder Brother cast his spells, he had Zhu San off to one side, drawing them out.

Third Brother didn't send Ouyang Jue to the front; he ordered him to stay in the warehouse. Once the battle began, he was rushed off his feet keeping the ledgers up to date as equipment was moved out. At that moment, he was glad he hadn't been able to get himself to the front line. The evidence of his own ears told him that this battle was quite different from any that had gone before. The battlefield was not over towards the Foreign Concession; it was right here, to the south of the city. Later, he discovered that the fighting had taken place around the Temple of Buddha's Light, and the villages of Balitai, Heiniucheng and Jizhuangzi.

He hoped that when the time came for the attack on the Foreign Concession, they would send him.

The battle became fiercer in the afternoon; sometimes, the sound of gunfire seemed to be coming from right in front of them.

One of the Militia members standing nearby told Ouyang Jue that the sound he could hear was actually the firing of shells. He could tell that the shells were landing not far away. Shortly after he said that, a couple of shells landed right in the middle of the village, exploding with a plume of thick smoke that hurled earth and plant material high into the sky. Luckily, none of these shells fell into the courtyard, but he could smell the strong scent of freshly-turned earth and plant clippings mixed in with the stench of gunpowder as it blew towards him, wave after wave. Later, a shell hit the grassy slope near the milling ground and exploded, leaving a crater the size of a house.

Ouyang Jue was struck speechless with fear when he saw the deep crater. If that shell had fallen anywhere near the hut where he worked on his ledgers, he would certainly have been killed. But the following day, a couple of Militia members were laughing their heads off as they lay at the bottom of the crater. They said it was really soft and warm down there – it felt as great as being snuggled up to their wives in bed.

That day, Ouyang Jue was much busier than usual. People kept charging up to him wanting guns, wanting bows, wanting arrows, wanting carrying poles, wanting punt guns, wanting gunpowder, wanting bandages for the wounded men, wanting medicine to stop them from bleeding or for pain relief – that was the "Dragon Bone" powder that Zhu San had smeared on his stomach the other day. Just judging from the constant demands for stuff to be issued, and how urgently the requests came in, you could imagine how fierce the battle raging outside the village must be. There had been so many engagements fought over the previous couple of days: there'd never been such demand for haemostatic medicines and bandages before. It was very frightening. Ouyang Jue couldn't help asking, "Is the fighting very fierce up ahead?"

"Even Master Liu is right out on the front line," said one Militia member, who'd come in to collect supplies.

Ouyang Jue had more questions, but suddenly he noticed a ray of light coming from the door. He turned around and saw that Third Brother was standing in the courtyard, looking at him with his head cocked to one side. He was so scared he immediately shrunk back, knowing that he had broken the rule of not asking questions. He buttoned his lip and bowed his head over his work.

Somewhat later, a huge guy holding a sword rode a black mule straight into the courtyard. He jumped off his mount and ran into the warehouse. The loops holding his vest together had been torn open, and there were rents across the chest, exposing his thick chest hair and deep-set navel. His clothing was spattered with blood. He slammed the sword down on the table with a bang and shouted to Ouyang Jue, "Give me all the Dragon Bone powder you've got. Elder Brother's been shot!" His voice was loud and menacing.

This news frightened everyone in the warehouse out of their wits.

When Ouyang Jue recovered himself, he quickly ran into the warehouse, pulled a large bag of haemostatic medicine from the shelf and gave it to him. The huge man picked it up and rushed away, riding his mule at a gallop.

At this point, Third Brother was not out in the courtyard. By the time he heard the news and came rushing over, the big man had already gone. Third Brother told someone to get him a couple of fast horses, and he set off at a gallop with one of the other young men. He was going to find out what had happened to Elder Brother.

This appalling fighting lasted for a day and a night; the sound of guns and rifles firing never let up. As the night wore on, people were coming to the warehouse to collect torches, flint strikers and lamplighters. No one was asking for weapons any more. They'd run out of medicine long ago; people said that Third Brother had sent someone over to the Grand Canal to ask Master Han for help. At daybreak, there was only the occasional sporadic burst of gunfire coming from out front. Without the sound of the guns, it seemed astonishingly depressing, particularly because there was no news about how the battle had gone – everyone was uneasy and on edge.

In the morning light, the distant plain was fringed with puffs of smoke, some light and some dense. The light smoke was nothing to worry about, but the thick smoke was absolutely terrifying.

No one was coming in any more demanding fresh supplies. The Militia members working in the warehouse were only worried about the results of this battle and whether Elder Brother was dead or alive. Everyone was exhausted. Ouyang Jue was so tired he fell asleep, slumped across his account books on the table. A few of the Militia members working in the warehouse simply could not stay awake, so they slept sprawled across hemp sacks stuffed with provisions. It wasn't until a bunch of men arrived with a dozen or so sacks of Dragon Bone powder from Master Han over at the Grand Canal that they woke up.

In the fighting yesterday, Master Han had sent out some of the toughest troops on the battlefield, and they'd suffered pretty heavy casualties. Even so, when he heard that Third Brother was asking for help, he'd insisted on sending over all these bags of Dragon Bone powder.

Once Ouyang Jue had seen Master Han's people off the premises, nothing happened for a long time. This quietness was hard to endure.

The sun gradually started to slant a little over to the west. Suddenly, the most amazing sound of drumming could be heard from outside the village, loud and clear. With this joyful music, the sound of gunfire finally came to an end. Afterwards, a crowd of Militia members returned to the village. The weather in June was already very hot, and they'd been fighting for twenty-four hours at a stretch, so they were all soaked in sweat, as wet as if they'd had jumped into a bath in their clothes. These victorious warriors were also liberally bespattered with blood, and some of them had removed their vests to reveal their darkly tanned torsos. As they marched along, they brandished their swords and shouted, at once overwhelmed with the excitement of victory and giving vent to the fear that they'd been holding back through all those long hours of fighting.

It was at that moment that they realised that this unimaginably, unprecedentedly bloody battle had been won.

You might have imagined that this news would be greeted with a massive celebration. They ought to be baking "Victory" cakes, cooking up sweet mung-bean soup, burning incense, thanking the gods and praying to the spirits, telling all kinds of tall tales about the killing of the foreigners. But until the setting sun turned the milling ground red, it remained silent and deserted. Then the drums and bugles on the southwest side of the village began to sound again, but it was not a joyful tune they were playing. Ouyang Jue could make out the wailing of the *suona* horn, the shriek of the *shengyu* pipes, the sad notes of the *erhu* spike fiddle and mournful beats of the drum. The Militia members stationed in Gao Family Village and the villagers themselves all crowded in together in the open space in front of the gate to Liu Nineteen's residence. They were there to hold a funeral for Elder Brother, who'd been killed in battle.

Ouyang Jue wasn't allowed to join them. From where he was standing, it was impossible to watch the progress of the funeral, but he could hear the dirges being played as the sun set in the west, followed by the mobile artillery battalions firing their guns into the sky. Ouyang Jue saw nothing of that amazing, earth-shattering scene; but he could see all the water birds that lived out in the wilderness flying off in alarm at the sound of the guns, wheeling through the cloudless, darkening evening sky.

All this time, Third Brother had been at Liu Nineteen's side, so he hadn't come back. One of the Militia members working in the warehouse whispered to Ouyang Jue that Third Brother and Elder Brother had both come from Shandong that spring with Master Liu. The two of them were landless peasants from the same village. They'd got caught up in a feud with some local Christians and had vowed to go to Tianjin and get rid of the Westerners who were supporting these bloody Chinese Christians no matter how much they bullied everyone else. Plenty of folk knew that Master Liu Nineteen's real name was Liu Chengxiang, but nobody seemed to have heard the names of Elder Brother and Third Brother. All that they knew was that Third Brother had been orphaned as a small child. Nobody seemed to know who his father was, and that his mother was starving when she'd given birth to him. She'd been screaming with pain, but nobody knew whether it was giving birth to him that was so painful, or whether it was the hunger. She'd died as soon as he was born, but nobody seemed to know whether she'd starved to death or it was childbirth that had killed her. Third Brother grew up like a wild dog; he survived on what he could pick up around the village. Elder Brother had looked after him. Nobody knew all the ins and outs of it, but everyone could understand that Elder Brother must have done something pretty impressive to help him out and that was what had made the two of them so close – so close that one would risk his life to save the other.

Ouyang Jue soon realised that almost half of the people who lived in the same courtyard as himself hadn't come back after the battle. There was one scout who hadn't come back; and of the four flag signalmen, only three had returned with their flags so shot to pieces that they had to ask some of the village women to help with patching them. The chubby cook from Wuqiang in Hebei Province had apparently been blown to pieces by a shell. Zhu San didn't come back either – was that because he was still over at the west side of the village? No one told him, and he couldn't ask. There was also a bugler from Linyi in Shandong Province called Liu Xiaoliu. Although he was still just a kid, he could play all kinds of instruments and sing too. He could make up songs on the spot – a likeable, mischievous and cheerful boy. He once made up a song and then sang it to Ouyang Jue. There were only four lines to his ballad:

> The Militia of Righteous Harmony will always fight;
> Turn around, step this way, and put yourself right!
> There's so much you can do when you have the might,
> While birds in the trees just sing to the light.

But the next morning, when the drummer came back, he just hung his head and cried. He said that Liu Xiaoliu had been shot in the stomach by the foreigners' bullets. In his agony, he'd been thrashing this way and that in the grass, turning over and over, but in the end they hadn't been able to save him.

The people in the courtyard sighed at this and did their best to comfort the drummer. Everyone knew that this drummer had been very close to the endlessly cheerful and optimistic Liu Xiaoliu. They'd always played music together, and when they weren't performing they were inseparable friends. Now he'd lost him, and he must feel as if he'd lost his right hand. One of the Militia members asked him, "Didn't he have a talisman when he went into battle?"

"Everyone was given a talisman after Elder Brother had cast his magic spells," the drummer explained. "Third Brother put Liu Xiaoliu's talisman on him personally."

"I thought if you wore a talisman, you couldn't be wounded by sword or gun…" the man said.

"Third Brother said it was because he hadn't learned martial arts properly," the drummer said. "If you get killed, it's either because you don't have good martial arts, or that you're not sincere. If you've trained properly and you really believe then the gods and spirits will possess you, and no bullet can come anywhere near you."

The Militia member was now even more confused and asked, "So how did Elder Brother die? He was great at martial arts!"

"Everyone says that today the foreigners were using some kind of demonic magic – they had women sitting naked on top of their cannons, and that broke our spirit possession!" the drummer said.

"Do foreigners cast spells too then?"

"Third Brother said next time we fight we'll be armed with a magical power that can break their devil-worshipping spells!" the drummer proclaimed.

The signaller, Meng Dashan, now said, "I've heard that over in Tianjin, Master Zhang has told everyone to put their womenfolk's bloody cloths into the chimney so that they don't get hit by the foreign devils' shells – it works really well."

"I've heard that Master Liu himself is going to go and pit his wits against the foreign devils in Zizhulin," the drummer said.

"That'll be the end of them!" the company all cried.

Although they spoke with great conviction, in their hearts nobody was quite sure any more that they were going to be victorious.

Two days later, Ouyang Jue was busy again. He had a hunch that Third Brother was preparing materiel for the next big battle. Ouyang Jue had not set eyes on Third Brother in person – he took his orders from the messengers he sent. All this time, he was by Liu Nineteen's side. After Elder Brother died, the division headquarters had moved west of the village to where Liu Nineteen was living. The morning and evening roll calls were also held out there. Ouyang Jue never saw Zhu San again. With Zhu San gone, there were some matters that he simply could not deal with because he didn't have the authority. He had to follow the instructions he received from Third Brother because he didn't dare decide for himself. But as two more days went by without any news of Zhu San, he began to wonder whether he too had been killed. Of course, he did not ask. There was a rule here: under no circumstances were you to enquire whether someone else was dead or alive. He also noticed that this time Third Brother wasn't bringing equipment in from outside and storing it in his warehouse; he was moving things from here to Liu Nineteen's headquarters. The warehouse was gradually being picked clean;. There was very little food left, and some of the Militia camped outside the village – who'd come here from various counties in Hebei Province – were starting to eat the famine foods that poor people survive on in bad years: "The three treasures of Weinanwa – knotroot, goosefoot greens and wild millet."

Ouyang Jue felt that after the fierce battle two days before, the power of the Militia at Gao Family Village had obviously shrunk, just like a strong man that has suddenly lost a whole lot of weight.

He suddenly considered: what if they are now no longer guarding the place so strictly? The thought of escape flashed again through his mind. But he didn't dare do anything hasty; he needed to investigate first.

He remembered the quiet road leading out from the back of the courtyard over the west of the village that he'd walked last time with Zhu San – he ought to go back there again to see if it was still as heavily guarded. Now that there were so many fewer people, would there not be holes in their defences? He found an opportunity to sneak off, and the road did indeed seem even quieter than last time. Carefully checking the whole place over, he could not see any sign of men on patrol. He thought: to begin with, a strict guard was being kept here, but now they've lost so many men that they must have had to reduce their patrols – this is my best chance of getting away. But even if he were able to escape from Gao Family Village, how was he to get to the Foreign Concession? At the moment, they were still fighting so fiercely; how could he possibly get to where he wanted to go? He didn't want to repeat his experience last time, when he'd nearly drowned in the mere.

Just as he was thinking it all over and hesitating about what to do for the best, he heard the sound of someone crying. He crouched down in silence; there it was again. He tiptoed over towards where the sound was coming from, getting gradually closer and closer. He cautiously raised himself and wriggled through a patch of scrubby woodland so that he could see who it was. There was a Militia member crying his heart out in among the trees, his head bowed. He had both hands up covering his face, and his shoulders were heaving. When his crying was at its most intense, he even started to wail – a heartbreaking sound.

The man stood up with his back turned. Nevertheless, Ouyang Jue suddenly recognised that vigorous physique – it was Third Brother! He was amazed: why would Third Brother be here all on his own crying? What could have happened to upset him so? Was this about the death of Elder Brother? Yes, of course; he would be mourning the death of his blood brother – Elder Brother was like family to him.

At this moment, the crying suddenly stopped. Third Brother stretched out his left arm, spread his fingers, slapped his hand down against the trunk of the tree in front of him, and then with a *swish* drew his sword with his right hand. With a silver flash, he brought the blade down on his left hand, cutting off his own little finger with a sharp snap. Before the blood had time to spurt out, he quickly undid a small bag of haemostatic medicine from his belt, plastered it onto his hand, and then bandaged the wound tightly with a piece of cloth.

It was all too unexpected and sudden. He moved so quickly, so violently, so decisively. At the same time, what he was doing was so bizarre. Ouyang Jue watched him with his mouth hanging open – he was dumbstruck! What happened next was even more peculiar: Third Brother bent over and searched the ground for the little finger he'd just cut off, and then he put it in his mouth and chewed on it, before swallowing it down!

Ouyang Jue was utterly appalled!

When Third Brother turned around, he could see that his eyes were so bloodshot they had gone bright red. An intense rage was making him grind his teeth with a horrible cracking sound, while the tendons in his cheeks were so taught it seemed they might snap. Third Brother didn't stop; he walked quickly out of the woods.

Ouyang Jue thought that if Third Brother had not been overcome with anger, he would certainly have been spotted – he was in such a state of shock that he was standing among the trees bolt upright, his head showing above the bushes. He was so close that Third Brother should have seen him at first glance.

He now had no intention of trying to escape, so he went scurrying back.

Ouyang Jue got back to the courtyard, and after finishing his work at the warehouse he came out again, only to discover Third Brother was sitting on the millstone in the courtyard waiting for him. That gave him a turn; he imagined that Third Brother had spotted him in the forest just now and had come to find him. He was worried: if Third Brother asked him what he had been doing in the forest, how should he reply?

But Third Brother's expression was exactly the same as usual. He just had his left hand wrapped up in a piece of cloth, and blood was oozing from his little finger. Without beating about the bush, Third Brother asked him outright, "Are you ready to do battle against the foreigners?"

Ouyang Jue was amazed, but he pulled himself together and answered, "I am not afraid to fight them."

"Why not?" Third Brother asked. "Don't the foreigners sell their paper to your family?"

"The colonial powers are occupying our country and using their guns to kill us," Ouyang Jue said. He didn't know why he said that. Was this what he really thought, or was he just saying it to please Third Brother?

His words made Third Brother raise his eyebrows and ask him another question. "Are you afraid to die?"

"My only fear is that I don't know any martial arts," Ouyang Jue said.

"As long as you're sincere, our spells will work," Third Brother said. Then, glancing at him, he gave an unexpected smile and said, "You look pretty clever, but you are also honest."

Ouyang Jue could tell that Third Brother actually quite liked him. He was flattered and surprised. He fell silent, simply because he didn't know what to say.

Suddenly, Third Brother announced, "You are now a member of the Militia." He raised his hand and threw something at Ouyang Jue.

When he opened it up, it turned out to be a piece of blue cloth. With this turban, he was formally enrolled in the Militia of Righteous Harmony. He felt a strange excitement.

Third Brother put out his hand, jumped down from the millstone and told him, "Prepare enough talismans to go round. Tomorrow morning, you'll join me in the attack on Zizhulin."

Ouyang Jue brightened. There was now no need for him to try to escape. Tomorrow, he'd be on his way.

CHAPTER 14

American troops from the Eight-Nation Alliance

OVER THE COURSE OF A LONG, long night, the burning heat of the day was gradually absorbed by the ground, but the smell of gun smoke remained. This pungent, stinging stench lingered, floating through the cool air at dawn.

Every sunrise, it is the heavens that wake up first as the sky brightens, when all living things on earth are still fast asleep, blanketed by the thick early morning mists. Thousands of Militia members, under cover of these all-enveloping mists, began to move in total silence in the direction of the southern edge of the Foreign Concession, advancing as fast as they could. Yesterday, Liu Nineteen and Zhang Decheng of 'Number One Division', Cao Futian of Kan Division and Teng Desheng of Li Division had met at the Temple to the Medicine King, east of the river, to discuss their next move. They decided to join forces in a united attack on the Zizhulin Concession. The "Number One Division" and the Kan Division were to launch a frontal assault from Majiakou; meanwhile, Liu Nineteen would cut off the Allied Army's retreat at the southern edge of the concession.

In Gengzi year of the reign of the Guangxu Emperor – 1900 in the Western calendar – the Zizhulin Concession was composed of four individual concessions. Travelling from north to south, there were the French, American, British and German Concessions. However, this war was not fought by troops from these four countries alone; Russia, Italy, the Austro-Hungarian Empire and Japan had also sent soldiers to join the campaign. Just as Old Master Ouyang had divined, these colonial powers were all hoping to profit from this opportunity to carve off some territory in Tianjin, and to plant their flags in the body of this huge, ageing Sick Man of Asia. Together, they formed the large and powerful Eight-Nation Alliance. Because of this alliance, the troops defending at the southern end of the concession would not necessarily be German soldiers.

Before dawn, Liu Nineteen mustered his forces. Having lost a number of men and horses in the Battle of Jizhuangzi a few days before, this time he was bringing in extra troops recruited from villages south and west of the city of Tianjin. The new peasant Militia members were grouped ten to a squad, and five squads made up a company. These men were quite different from the real soldiers. They were all farm boys who'd normally be working in the fields in times of peace; but now that war had broken out, they'd come to join the fighting. Liu Nineteen was an extraordinarily charismatic leader; his call for troops had elicited a massive response, and today he'd gathered at least three thousand new recruits to add to their forces.

When the Militia went into battle, there was no clear formation – they moved like a herd of sheep, milling around in roughly the same direction. Ouyang Jue was following along behind Third Brother. This was the first time he'd ever been in a battle, and his heart was thumping. Actually, he had no intention of doing any fighting; his plan was to run away at the first opportunity, but that prospect made him even more nervous than he otherwise might have been.

When they had gone about ten miles from Gao Family Village, they reached an area of wilderness with no sign of life. In among this wasteland, there were vast areas of marsh, reed-fringed ponds, and endless hillocks covered in scrub and thickets of trees. It looked just like the place where he'd been a couple of weeks earlier when he'd attempted to make his way out to the Foreign Concession alone, only to fall into a pond and then get captured by the Boxers. In fact there were many places that looked familiar. That time, he'd been lost, so he'd struggled around one obstacle after another with immense difficulty with no idea where he was going; this time, they had local guides who made the whole journey much easier – they weren't wading through the mere or struggling through mud, nor did they have to keep making detours. Pretty soon, a frieze of buildings rose up before their eyes: they had reached the Foreign Concession.

An order came back that the scouts had already gone out to locate where the foreigners were lurking. They were to lie in ambush and wait until the Brothers gave the order to move. Immediately, more than a thousand Militia members lay down and hid in the grass, waiting with bated breath. There was no sign of movement over in the Foreign Concession; clearly, they had not been spotted. Ouyang Jue thought that the Militia was really amazing in the way that they could move their men from place to place in complete silence, to attack out of the blue.

Before they'd even set out from Gao Family Village, Third Brother had pasted a talisman onto the sword of each one of his men. He said, "The spell has now entered your weapon – all you have to do is attack! The enemy will be helpless!" Third Brother had also pasted a talisman onto Ouyang Jue's stomach to render him invulnerable to foreign bullets. After it had been affixed, he slapped the paper hard twice over. Having this mysterious amulet about his person really did make him feel so much braver. Third Brother had been very kind to him. But now as he squatted down in the grass, he was not thinking about killing foreigners; he was going to find Xénia. He was wondering, after so many days had gone by, would Xénia still be waiting for him in the little white building?

Now that they were at war and the concession had become so dangerous, had her father sent her back to Europe? After all, her home wasn't here in the Foreign Concession but far away in France. He remembered the lovely photographs of her as a child he'd seen when he'd visited her house.

Thinking of this, although he remained hopeful, it seemed that the situation was slipping further and further from his grasp.

A shot startled Ouyang Jue awake. All this time, the lot of them had been keeping their heads down, concealed amid the grass. Now they lifted their heads, they could see the sky was very bright. A line of foreign buildings – grey and white, high and low – appeared ahead of them, not far away. He could even see people moving around on top of the buildings. Some Westerners with guns were perched atop the walls and up on the roofs.

Third Brother, lying in ambush up ahead of them, suddenly shouted, "Kill!"

Immediately, the drums sounded the attack. The sound came from somewhere ahead of them, over to the right; Ouyang Jue had not even noticed when the drummers moved into position there.

The cries of "Kill!" rose up, as if erupting from the ground. The Militia members, lying in ambush in the grass, leapt to their feet. As countless men ran forward, their blue turbans fluttering, their broadswords flashing with a silver light, in the blink of an eye this wilderness was turned into a turbulent sea – the blue was the waters and the silver the foam on the top of the waves pouring towards the Foreign Concession. Ouyang Jue was propelled forward by this heroic momentum, as if he were caught in a powerful current that dragged him along with it involuntarily. As the drums and clappers beat vigorously, he too shouted and waved his broadsword. He could see a number of the Militia's triangular flags with red saw-toothed edges carried forward in the vanguard, speeding like arrows. Soon, they would reach the concession.

However, a barrage of bullets fired from the buildings opposite them quickly felled the Militia members rushing forward so passionately. Almost all of the men on the front line were killed on the spot.

They couldn't even see the foreigners' lines.

However, the soldiers who were stationed in the buildings opposite them were well-trained and orderly. Someone gave the signal with a whistle, and the shooting began immediately afterwards.

The moment the Militia of Righteous Harmony attempted to storm the concession, the whistling would sound, and then after a volley of shots a line of men would fall. Then, another group would charge forward, there would be another whistle, and again they would be cut down. Soon, the plain out in front of the Foreign Concession was covered with heaps of corpses, lying higgledy-piggledy all over the place.

The Militia were definitely the losers when they fought the foreigners. The Westerners had guns; they could shoot the Boxers dead from a long way away. The Militia of Righteous Harmony had swords; they could only kill people if there was hand-to-hand fighting. But they never even got close; they were being shot dead long before they got within spitting distance of the foreigners.

The Militia members ran forward, brandishing swords and clubs, only for their attack to be brought to a halt by the foreigners' bullets – they had no choice but to seek cover. But out there on that vast plain, there was nothing to hide behind. Furthermore, the Westerners perched up in their coigns of vantage could see their every move. They could treat the Boxers out in the wilderness as target practice; having picked one out, they would aim, fire and shoot the man dead. The Militia was helpless. It seemed that the foreigners could kill any one of them the moment they felt like it. A heavy-set bearded man was crouching down, close to the ground. He couldn't stand the humiliation. All of a sudden, he jumped up screaming, swinging his broadsword with rings set in the blade through the air and shouting curses. He rushed forward all by himself, but before he'd gone more than a few paces he was struck by a bullet aimed directly at him, and he fell to the ground in a welter of blood.

The Militia members could now see just how powerful the foreigners' guns really were, and no one wanted to die. They crouched down out on the plain, quite motionless.

The foreigners began to fire their cannons in their direction. Shells were falling right on top of where the Militia were positioned. A couple of men were being blasted into the air with each explosion. There was absolutely nothing they could do; they had to take this beating – the foreigners simply cut them to pieces.

At this time, more than a dozen men suddenly came hurrying past Ouyang Jue. The man walking in front turned around and looked at him. Ouyang Jue recognised him: it was Third Brother. However, on this occasion, his face was frighteningly grim and his eyes were as bloodshot as they had been that day when he cut off his finger in the woods. He told Ouyang Jue, "Come with me..."

Ouyang Jue showed his hesitation; he didn't move. Third Brother cursed him angrily. "Arsehole!" After that he ignored him, moving off quickly, the rest of his men in tow.

In that instant, a shell came whistling over and landed right next to Third Brother. The explosion was so enormous that Ouyang Jue was blasted off his feet before he could understand what had happened to him. When he crawled out of the loose earth and debris kicked up by the explosion, he looked around for Third Brother, but he had disappeared.

Third Brother must have been killed by the shell exploding, but the strange thing was that there was no body.

Ouyang Jue looked everywhere, but it was nowhere to be seen. What could have happened? Had Third Brother been blown to bits?

Had his body been sent flying? Was there nothing left? How could that be possible? Where could he have gone?

Ouyang Jue was stunned, and so were the other Militia members. They called out to Third Brother at the tops of their voices, but there was no response. Third Brother was dead; but more than that, he was dead and gone – every trace of him had been wiped off the earth.

The blue sky stretched above their heads, completely empty. There was just a thin, lingering line of glittering smoke, light and insubstantial.

It all seemed quite unbelievable. Had he vanished into thin air just like this thread of smoke? Had he been translated like an immortal?

In this sad moment, there was no one to take command. All the Militia members present simply knelt down together, facing towards the southeast. They did not appear to even notice the constant bombardment, nor did they seem to be frightened at the prospect of being blown to pieces by the shells whizzing overhead – everyone just stayed kneeling down on the ground, motionless, their faces turned towards the southeast. It seemed they were prepared to die alongside Third Brother.

Any moment now, they would be massacred by the foreigners.

At this moment, they heard the sound of horses' hooves galloping as a band of men rode up, screaming and shouting "Kill! Kill them all!" in murderous tones.

The Militia members kneeling on the ground looked back; it was Liu Nineteen's mobile artillery battalions. Ouyang Jue had no idea where they could have sprung from; they seemed to appear out of nowhere. Each one of them was on horseback, dressed entirely in dark blue, but with sky-blue turbans wrapped round their heads and heavy boots on their feet. They were armed with blunderbusses, Western-style rifles, punt guns, long shotguns, five-barrel machine guns or hand cannons; and every single one of them carried on his back a steel sword with a red tassel hanging from the pommel.

Ouyang Jue was able to make out that their leader was riding a bay horse. Its head was covered by a chanfron, with red strips of cloth arranged in a cross-hatched pattern. He remembered that one of the grooms who'd lived in the same courtyard had mentioned that Master Liu Nineteen rode a bay horse given to him by Hitara Hala Yulu, the governor of Zhili Province, and that he had his mount kitted out in a caparison decorated with red cross-hatching. It was Liu Nineteen himself! It must be him! He wanted to see the face of the man riding the bay horse, but he rode like the wind, so fast that he couldn't even be sure if he was wearing a scarf covering his face or not. But in that flash when Liu Nineteen galloped past him, Ouyang Jue got a clear view of his figure. Although he was not tall, his shoulders were surprisingly wide, square and flat, and they were cocked, like an owl's. Behind him, a dark blue cape streamed out in the wind. He looked majestic, cold and stern.

He sat like a god on that beautiful bay horse, striking fear into the hearts of all who saw him!

Few people ever got to see Liu Nineteen, but Ouyang Jue was one of them. Although he only ever set eyes on Liu Nineteen this one time, and even then all he got to see was his back, how many people could claim to have even caught a glimpse of this remarkable man?

Liu Nineteen shook the reins, and his horse flew forward.

He rode at the head of his mobile artillery battalions, and they followed along behind him.

Braving the constant hail of bullets, they charged fearlessly into the Foreign Concession straight ahead of them.

The Militia rank and file, who only moments before had been pinned down on that vast expanse of wilderness, now clambered to their feet, screaming and shouting, running in the wake of the mobile artillery battalions, pouring into the Foreign Concession like a tidal wave. From in the front of the Western buildings, there came confused sounds of the sharp scrape of blades, gunfire, screaming, killing...

Nobody knows what happened after that.

There was only one person left lying out there in the grass, and that was Ouyang Jue. For a moment, he didn't know where to go – he was feeling deeply confused.

He had been scared out of his wits by a series of incredible events, and his head was in a whirl. Third Brother had been killed by an exploding shell, leaving no body behind – how bizarre was that? Of course, there'd been his own hesitation and refusal to step forward, as well as Third Brother's angry disappointment and his own shame. Then there had been the Militia of Righteous Harmony's suicidal attempt to charge when the foreigners' guns were cutting them down without mercy. Which would win: Western firepower or the Militia's magical spells and martial arts? And then there was his passing encounter with Liu Nineteen; what he had seen there was the back view of a nonpareil hero. Never in his entire life had he encountered a man who was so truly awe-inspiring!

Caught up as he was in these confused and strange feelings, his aim remained clear – he wanted to get back to the little white building. However, his feelings about his aim had already changed. After all that had happened in the last few weeks, he had moved beyond his original uncomplicated desire and yearning for Xénia. What had once been a natural expression of passion had gradually faded away. Now all that was left was a kind of unresolved emotional entanglement...

For some reason, the closer he got to the little white house, the more remote from Xénia he felt. For many days now, he had lurched from one strange and bizarre event to another, meeting each of them head-on. It had all been totally unanticipated; none of this was anything he had intended, and he'd suffered continuous bad luck. He had no idea what to expect next! He simply could not begin to imagine what might overtake him. He could feel that more misfortunes lay in store, but as to what they might be, he could not say.

Where should he go now? Did he still want to go to that small white building? Yes, he was still determined to go there. Even if it was just to put an end to the whole thing, to see her for the last time, to say goodbye forever to that beautiful blue-eyed girl.

Ouyang Jue stumbled forward.

In recent years the Foreign Concession had been undergoing expansion and development, and the boundary line now wiggled in and out. As a result, it was possible to make your way into the concession between pretty much any of the buildings. Because of this, any and all of the houses that touched the boundary line could be part of the foreigners' fortifications. It was impossible to say which of these buildings had troops lying in ambush inside, and you might come under fire at any moment. There were a couple of occasions when he could hear a bullet come whistling past him, but he had no idea which of the buildings it had been fired from. If any one of those bullets had hit him, he'd have been killed instantly.

To begin with, he was hiding and trying to seek cover, but afterwards he didn't bother – the bullets didn't come flying any more either. He was quite surprised at this; did that mean that the talisman Third Brother had given him really worked? But in that case, why had Third Brother himself been blown to pieces by a shell? Didn't he know all kinds of magic spells and incantations? Had he been overpowered by the foreigners' demonic arts like Elder Brother? He couldn't understand it. He'd never been in a battle before, let alone a battle fought with Western rifles and cannons.

Clearly, the all-out war between Zizhulin and the old city was now underway. He could hear the booming of guns in all directions. Ever since he'd looked at the old city through Xénia's telescope, he had a relatively clear sense of the direction and orientation of the walls with respect to his current location within the Foreign Concession. He knew the spots far in the distance where he could see the smoke rising were the old city, the southern suburbs, the junction of the three rivers and the eastern bank of the White River; then even further away, there was Beidaguan. Smoke was rising all over the concession too, and fires were raging in some places. The blocks that had just been attacked by Liu Nineteen and his mobile artillery were now burning fiercely – bright tongues of flame licking through the thick black smoke. The longest tongues were as much as ten metres high, making it seem that they were licking at the sky. Smoke was also rising over several of the open depressions in the wilderness on the north side of Hai Avenue, where exploding shells had set fire to the weeds and scrub – evidently, there was also fighting going on out there. Puff after puff of gun smoke mixed with the smell of myriad burning things floated towards him on the hot winds of summer. He could see that not far ahead of him, a group of Militia members in red turbans were charging the Foreign Concession, screaming at the tops of their voices. There was volley after volley of gunshots, but they continued to charge forward suicidally. Although men were constantly being shot down, in the end they were able to charge into the concession. Knowing that there was fighting immediately ahead of him, Ouyang Jue hid behind a pile of reeds and waited for the gunfire to die down a little before proceeding. Later on, he realised that out there in the wilderness he was far too exposed, so he changed the way he was moving; he would run straight over to the front of one of the buildings and flatten himself against it, skirting the building itself or its perimeter wall. That was obviously a lot safer – he wasn't being shot at any more by the snipers.

As he made his way past a small group of Western buildings, he saw many corpses scattered across the street lying in terrible pools of bright red blood. Most of the corpses were red-turbaned members of the Militia of Righteous Harmony, but there were also two or three foreign soldiers. Most of the Militia members had been shot dead, while all the foreigners had been hacked to pieces. Just one glance would tell you that horrific fighting had recently taken place here.

Ouyang Jue was about to pass by when all of a sudden, a man grabbed him. He was holding a sword, so he turned around instinctively and tried to cut the man down, but he didn't know how to use his weapon. This made it easy for the man to grab his arm and drag him off into the courtyard of one of the foreign buildings nearby.

When Ouyang Jue looked at the man, he turned out to be a Boxer. His clothes were stained with blood, and a talisman was pasted in the middle of his headscarf. The eyes below that headscarf were open wide, showing an expression of surprise. Just as he'd come to the conclusion that the man looked a little familiar, he called out, "Second Young Master, it's you! You've joined the Militia too!"

In his confusion, he simply could not think who it could be. The man yanked his headscarf down and said, "Second Young Master, it's me, Wei Xiaosan!"

Ouyang Jue was both surprised and pleased. He exclaimed, "It's you! It's really you! Since you're here, can you tell me what's happened to my family – my father, my elder brother and my wife? Tell me!"

An embarrassed, troubled expression crossed Wei Xiaosan's face. He said, "After the young master shut down the business, I joined the Militia of Righteous Harmony."

"But you must know how my family is, surely!"

"I don't know what's happened to them recently. Your family was fine a while back. Old Master Ouyang was fine, and your wife and the eldest young master were fine too. Of course, they were almost out of their minds with worry looking for you. They'd never have imagined you'd joined the Militia of Righteous Harmony. Why on earth would you do a thing like that?"

Ouyang Jue couldn't explain. He just asked the things he really wanted to know. Wei Xiaosan was always well informed and liked to talk. No matter what question you put to him, you'd get a ton of information, most of which wasn't anything you wanted to know. But if you kept on asking, you might hear of things you could never even have imagined.

Wei Xiaosan told him that on the same day as he'd disappeared, a strange thing happened at the Gongnan paper shop. When he got up in the morning and started to move the shutters, he found a small square piece of paper had been slipped underneath the door, with the word "tomorrow" written on it. There were a few other scribblings on the reverse, which looked like some kind of foreign language. He'd shown it to the other clerks in the store, but nobody understood what it meant; some of them thought that a child might have poked it in for a joke. But then a couple of days later, another piece of paper was slipped in, and this time it read "yes", which made even less sense.

"Did you see who put this little piece of paper under the door?" Ouyang Jue asked.

"Why, who could it be?" Wei Xiaosan enquired.

"I want to know. Did you see the person who slipped these papers under the door?"

"I have no idea who it was!" Wei Xiaosan replied. "He was putting the papers under the door overnight – by morning he was gone!"

"Did you show them to the eldest young master?" Ouyang Jue asked again.

Wei Xiaosan said that at that time, the eldest young master was rushed off his feet. He came and went from the store in such a hurry that he couldn't remember whether he'd mentioned it to him or not. The city was in chaos, and there were all kinds of rumours doing the rounds – all sorts of weird things were happening. A lot of shops were being robbed, and there were endless muggings. Who would care about a couple of bits of paper? It was just a little odd, that's all. Later on, the eldest young master had closed down both the Gongnan and the Guyi stores, and after that they hadn't found any more pieces of paper.

Ouyang Jue believed that Xénia must have been so desperate that she decided to risk all and come to the old city to find him. She would have gone on her own. How on earth had she managed to make her way from the Foreign Concession all the way to Gongnan Avenue? Why had she come during the night to slip pieces of paper under the door of the shop? Maybe she was trying to avoid attracting attention, or maybe it was because during the day, the roads were under strict guard... She'd come several times after all! Wasn't it silly of her to have imagined that she could use these squares of paper to communicate with him? But then, what else could she do?

One of the things Wei Xiaosan told him afterwards was truly appalling. Although this was just a rumour he'd heard and not something he'd seen with his own eyes, he'd been told about it after he joined the Militia of Righteous Harmony, and Ouyang Jue was quite sure it was true...

Apparently, a foreign woman had appeared on Gongqian Avenue one day, wandering up and down the road. She'd been captured by some Kan Division Militia members and locked up in a cage by the gate to the bannermen commander-in-chief's yamen.

Some people said that this foreign woman was a spy who'd come out from the Foreign Concession to get military intelligence. Others claimed that she was the witch who sat naked on top of the enemy's guns to cast her demonic spells. That brought a lot of people out to stand around the cage by the commander-in-chief's yamen to stare at the "foreign witch". Some of them were there to see something new; some were there to enjoy the spectacle; some of them were idle young men who'd turned up to tease and make fun of her; some poked and prodded at her; some lifted up her skirt with bamboo poles; and some of them used wooden batons to stab viciously at the witch's private parts. The foreign woman had screamed and shouted and cried, and then in the end she'd just seemed to go insane, tearing her hair and clawing at her face. With her hair hanging down and blood dripping everywhere, she'd looked absolutely terrifying.

"What happened next?" Ouyang Jue demanded loudly. "Where is she now?"

Wei Xiaosan couldn't understand why the second young master looked so terrible when he asked this question. He said that one night, the foreign woman suddenly disappeared. The following day when people looked, they saw that the door of the cage was open and the chains were lying on the ground. Some folk said that the Militia of Righteous Harmony had cut her head off; others said that the government had escorted her out of the Daying Gate under cover of darkness and sent her back to the concession because they were afraid her presence would give the foreigners an excuse to launch an all-out attack on the city. There were all kinds of stories, but no one had seen with their own eyes what had really happened to her.

As Wei Xiaosan was talking, Ouyang Jue kept asking more questions. Wei Xiaosan was on stuttering over his words, trying to get it all out.

All of this was just gossip and rumour. The one thing was that he'd heard that the foreign witch had "ghostly blue eyes" – that detail made Ouyang Jue quite sure that it was Xénia, but he couldn't provide any further information. He didn't even know when any of this had happened.

As Wei Xiaosan was talking, he realised that Ouyang Jue's expression was not right; he might have been on the edge of laughter or on the verge of tears – he looked very strange, and he did not understand why. So he talked about all sorts of things that he shouldn't have done and which had nothing to do with the second young master, and then he stopped. He wanted to ask if there was anything he could do for the second young master, but just as he opened his mouth, Ouyang Jue waved him away, telling him to leave. No matter what he said, the second young master just gestured at him to go, insisting that he should get away as quickly as he could.

At this time, it was up to each individual whether they lived or died; nobody had time to help anyone else. Wei Xiaosan had no choice but to go. Before leaving, he gave all the dry food he had with him to the second young master.

After Wei Xiaosan had gone, Ouyang Jue was left squatting alone in the empty building. He did not know how long he stayed there. All he could think about were confused images of Xénia. She no longer looked the way she had before: pure, beautiful, charming, tender, sincere and devoted. Instead, she appeared pitiful, helpless, innocent, suffering, humiliated and insane – all of this was how he imagined her. But for some reason, his imagination dwelt on her in the most terrible, the most humiliating, the most desperate, and the most unbearable situations.

He lamented, grieved, raged and mourned for her. He thought that if he had been there, he would have saved her even if it cost him his own life. He would have been happy to be humiliated with her in that cage. He would have been willing to die for her. He would have spoken up on her behalf: she is no spy! She is just a perfectly ordinary foreign girl. But all of this was useless. Everything had already happened.

And at a time like this, who would understand? Who would have taken responsibility for letting her go?

As things had transpired, just as he'd left the old city and rushed off to the Foreign Concession to find her, Xénia had been foolish enough to rush over to the old city again and again to try and find him. Even as he'd held to the conviction that she would wait for him over in that little white building, she'd been suffering the teasing of those ignorant people and every humiliation the dregs of society could think to mete out to her in the cage outside the entrance to the commander-in-chief's yamen. When he was trying every trick in the book to get away and meet her, she had already vanished without a trace. Who had arranged this absurd tragedy that would see them separated by life and death? Who would play with them so deliberately and cruelly? Why?

Where was Xénia now? Had she vanished from the face of the earth like Third Brother when he was hit by the shell? She must have died long before now.

Did this mean that none of this should have happened? Was it all over?

Ouyang Jue gradually calmed down. He still couldn't understand what had happened to him, or even believe it.

There was no need for him to go to that small white building ever again. Nothing else would ever happen there. Sooner or later, the weeds of time would cover it entirely.

It was time for him to go home.

CHAPTER 15

Public execution of Boxer soldiers

HE HAD LOST all track of time, to the point where he didn't know any more whether it was day or night. All that was left to him was a sense of direction; the old city was somewhere ahead of him, far in the distance. The enormous walls looked like a rotting old ship, beached upon the sands.

Tianjin had experienced many weeks of drought now, with not a drop of rain. During the day, the parching sun shone painfully bright in a clear blue sky, but once the guns started firing and everything was being blasted to smithereens, smoke filled the air. That made everything look different right away.

The fighting today was very unusual. When it began, it was very fierce, as if both sides had agreed to kill each other to the last man as quickly as possible. In the Foreign Concession, all the way along Hai Avenue, there was constant, relentless gunfire; guns were also being fired from the warships moored in the White River. In the dazzling sunlight, you could see the shells glittering as they flew over your head in an endless stream, falling to the ground inside and outside the city walls. At the same time, the seven Qing artillery batteries over in the old city were firing back. But with the exception of the powerful German Krupp guns off to the northeast, in the battery by the naval camp at the junction of the three rivers, as well as those mounted in the Lutai and Grand Canal batteries, the other cannons were inflicting nothing like the damage done by the shelling coming from the Allied Army in the Foreign Concession.

Somewhat over an hour later, the old city was rocked by a huge explosion. Nobody could understand what could have blown up with such a bang. A column of dense, roiling smoke rose up into the air, before spreading out into an enormous black mushroom cloud. It appeared right in front of Ouyang Jue and quickly spread out, like a drop of thick black ink dispersing in water, enveloping the old city in the most horrifying way. The sky above the old city immediately became dark, heavy and terrible. At this moment, the sound of gunfire merged into one continuous boom so that even the earth was constantly shaking.

Later on, he realised that this was the moment when troops

from the Eight-Nation Alliance began their attack on the city of Tianjin. It was the eighteenth of June 1900.

Exactly forty years earlier, Britain and France had conquered this city and then gone on to attack Beijing and burn the Old Summer Palace to the ground.

Tianjin people over the age of fifty were always frightened by the sound of foreign guns firing. They were not expecting that this time it would be even more violent, a much more destructive battle that would overwhelm the entire city. The enormous and powerful Eight-Nation Alliance Army was very much a rag-tag bunch; no one had any idea which country the troops attacking the city came from. The oddly-shaped flags and different uniforms made the inhabitants of Tianjin feel utterly confused.

Before returning to the city, so as not to be treated as a target, Ouyang Jue dumped his turban, sash and broadsword in one of the foreign buildings in the concession. As he crossed the wasteland, he bumped into a column of foreign cavalry, galloping along on horseback. This regiment was very strong – at least two or three thousand in total – and they charged into the old city in an unstoppable black stream. These cavalrymen were wearing pipe-like shakos and long dark coats. When they whipped their horses up to a gallop, they screamed and waved their heavy sabres. A couple of the cavalrymen spotted him, plucked the long guns off their backs and shot at him. As the bullets came whistling over, he fell flat on the ground, his head thrust into the grass. Fortunately, the real target of this cavalry was up ahead, so they had no interest in whether any one individual was alive or dead, and soon they had galloped by.

Ouyang Jue subsequently ran into another group of infantry soldiers, wearing huge round hats with very high tops, making them look like giant mushrooms. They fell on him like a group of hunters on a hare; some dropped down on one knee and started shooting at him, while others just stood there firing their rifles. He made haste to pretend to have been shot and fell down. These foreign soldiers were quite a distance away, so they didn't bother to come over and check; they just turned around and left. He was very lucky that they just walked on by. From this, he came to understand how to survive on the battlefield: lying flat on the ground playing dead. The best way to pretend to be dead was to lie face up, your eyes closed and your body quite still – that looked much more realistic than lying sprawled face down on the ground.

The purpose of war is to kill the enemy. If that was the way they wanted it, he could play dead with the best of them.

This time, he chose to take the route leading from Hai Avenue to the Daying Gate. A handful of villages were located out there, but this was not the main battlefield. Furthermore, there were all sorts of places where you could hide yourself, and that made it much safer than walking across the big, open depressions in the wilderness. The villages here were abandoned and empty, the doors to the houses hanging open. The inhabitants had all fled; some of the houses had been hit by shells, while others had gone up in flames. In and around these villages, there were many dead bodies to be seen; the majority of them were Boxers, their heads wrapped in either red or yellow turbans. He was shocked at the sight. He had no idea that so many members of the Militia of Righteous Harmony had been killed. What surprised him even more was that most of the dead had yellow paper talismans stuck on their swords or pasted in the middle of their turbans.

Through the gap in his half-opened vest, he could see a corner of the talisman stuck to his own stomach, peeling up like an old plaster. It had been put on him by Third Brother.

He pulled it off and threw it away.

Ouyang Jue entered a small village, shaded by numerous trees, which seemed very quiet. He wanted to find some water to drink. He was feeling very hot, hungry and thirsty. He'd taken some dry biscuits with him when he left Gao Family Village, and when Wei Xiaosan said goodbye to him, he also gave him all the food he had in the bag hanging from his belt. He didn't lack for food, but he needed water. It was just too hot. His mouth was dry, and his tongue felt like a piece of old shoe-leather. He simply couldn't sweat; he'd sweated himself dry and now felt as if he were burning to a crisp. It was as if his skin were just about to split, and when he ran his hand down himself, it was like touching a red-hot iron pot. He knew that there must be water somewhere in the village: wells are always found around where people live. He spotted a well in the village, but there was no bucket or rope to draw water. Luckily, in one low room, he found a broken tank, which was more than half full of water. Like an animal, he lowered his head and drank until his stomach bulged as tight as a drum, and yet he still felt thirsty. He jumped into the tank and washed himself all over – that finally brought his temperature down.

All of a sudden, there was a huge bang as a shell exploded; it sounded as if it had fallen right beside him. Ouyang Jue ran out into the courtyard and found no one there. The perimeter walls around each of the village houses were pretty low, so you could look right across. Three foreigners were in the next courtyard firing from the ruins of the house there. Hidden behind the tumbledown house, they had positioned a black iron gun on a wheeled undercarriage. They were methodically loading shells into the gun, firing again and again in the direction of the old city. They were chatting to one another as they fired the gun, and one of them was smoking. The three men were wearing boaters, with silk ribbons tied around them. It was so hot that they had taken off their coats and put them on the ruins of the wall, now reduced to half its original height. He had no idea which country these soldiers came from. Ouyang Jue was afraid of being discovered, so he quickly left the courtyard and ran out of the village, skirting the walls as closely as he could. He had just left the village when he ran straight into a small group of people. He was quite sure that they were going to kill him, but it turned out they were Chinese – they were unloading a cart piled high with wooden crates onto two-wheeled trolleys. The crates were filled with round black melon-like shells. These Chinese men were all wearing vests. They were working so hard that the sweat had soaked through, front and back. This sudden encounter gave everyone a turn. He was wondering how on earth they could be helping the foreigners by delivering shells to them, when one of them asked him, "What are you doing here?"

"I've just come from the Foreign Concession," Ouyang Jue said, "and I'm trying to get back to the old city."

"Aren't you scared to go over there?" the man said. "Don't you know that the attack is happening today? The Allied Army already have the city surrounded and they are firing guns into the city from every side."

"If you go back there," one of the others said, "aren't you just going to get yourself killed?"

"What am I to do?" Ouyang Jue exclaimed. "My family are all over there."

"Wait until the Allied Army has taken the city, then go back. I guess you're a Christian too, so you might as well give us a hand. We're all volunteers," the first man to speak to him explained.

Ouyang Jue saw that he was very thin, with tiny eyes – he reminded him a little of Mr Ma, but a good bit younger. "No," he said, "I'm worried about my family back home. I'll be fine as long as I'm careful." With that, he continued walking towards the old city of Tianjin.

He could hear the voices of the men behind him:

"Just wait until the Allied Army has captured Tianjin…"

"Shells don't care who they kill…"

"Your family may not be inside the city at all. Pretty much everyone fled before this started…"

This last sentence did give him pause for thought. Had everyone run away? What about his own family? He was afraid that if his family was still inside the city, they would fall victim to the Allied Army's artillery. If they had gone, he would not find them when he went back. But he had to go. Whatever happened, at least they would all be together.

Ouyang Jue had almost made it as far as the city walls when he was halted by a hail of bullets. He could go no further as there was a fierce battle raging there.

Far in the distance, he could see the foreigners' violent assault on the city; shells were raining down ceaselessly on the battered old walls. The Qing soldiers were crouched behind the crenellations, shooting at them through the embrasures. Apart from a few of the Boxers who were armed with fowling pieces, fighting side by side with the Qing Army, most members of the Militia of Righteous Harmony didn't have guns. They were being cut to pieces in the shelling, and corpses were strewn everywhere in front of the walls. The East Gate had already been blown open by the foreigners' shells and was burning. Fierce flames and thick smoke filled the entranceway. No one could possibly get through there.

Ouyang Jue decided to go first to the paper shop in Gongnan Avenue and hide there for a bit. He struggled through cloud after cloud of black and yellow gun smoke to make his way as far as Gongnan Avenue; but what he saw when he got there was so terrible he couldn't bear to look. Most shops on both sides of the street were destroyed, either blown apart or burnt out. His own family's 'Broadlight' paper shop had suffered the fate his father had most feared – it had gone up in flames, and the embers were still smouldering. It must have burned for many days already, since it was no longer giving off any smoke. Half of the Jade Beauties store, which sold such beautiful silk flowers, had gone as well.

What about the store on Guyi Street? What about his home? He couldn't bear to think about it.

Ouyang Jue hid in between a couple of broken-down walls. None of the tall buildings had survived anywhere, so you could now see a long way. He noticed that the two huge flagpoles in front of the Temple to the Queen of Heaven were all right; it seemed almost miraculous that they were still standing. The theatre opposite them was also undamaged, but he could not see if the Temple to the Queen of Heaven was safe. But not far away, the old city had become like an enormous coal-burning stove, belching out vast amounts of black smoke, curling up into the sky, shading the sun, darkening the scene before your very eyes. At that time, the shells fired by the Allied Army from beyond the walls continued to fly like locusts, falling into the old city in a never-ending stream. This spectacle made him feel that this was the end of the world. Now, his only hope was that his father and the rest of his family had indeed run away. If only when he went back all he would find was an empty house under the old scholar tree!

At that moment, he truly understood why people said that peace is the greatest blessing any human can enjoy.

The assault on the city lasted until the following day. Ouyang Jue spent the night squatting down between these crumbling walls. When he made his way back in front of the city wall, the shelling had finally come to an end. He couldn't hear explosions anywhere nearby. Now that the guns had stopped, he felt almost as if there were something missing.

Ouyang Jue stood on the wooden bridge across a moat outside the eastern walls, facing the barbican. It was as if he had arrived at the Gates of Hell. He didn't dare look at the corpses lying everywhere; instead, he fixed his gaze on the gatehouse, now missing its roof and wreathed in black smoke, and the city wall, damaged by the shelling and cratered with bullet holes. The stone plaque hanging above the gate, reading "Guarding the East", had been broken in two, and even worse, there were a bunch of flags flying over the walls, their eye-catching colouring shining bright in the sunlight. On one side, there was a white flag – who knows who had put that up there – and then the other three were the flags of the occupying forces: the United States, France and Japan. His elder brother, Ouyang Zun, had once taught him the flags of different foreign countries, so he could recognise most of them.

The barbican had been turned into a slaughterhouse by the victors.

This was the first time in his life that Ouyang Jue had ever seen executions being carried out. There were Boxers kneeling down on the ground; one executioner would hold their queue out in front to make them stretch their necks out, and then the second executioner behind them would raise his sword, bringing it down with a sharp swish to cut off the victim's head. Most of the people waiting to be beheaded were Boxers, but there were also some Qing soldiers. What shocked him even more was that there was now a fringe of human heads hanging from the top of the city walls, some three metres above him. There must have been seventy or eighty of them; other than a couple of Qing soldiers, the vast majority were Boxers – rank and file and also leadership. Some of them still had their turbans on. The occupying forces were establishing their authority with the reek of blood, and Ouyang Jue could feel the hairs prickling on the back of his neck.

Only a handful of people were inside the barbican – foreign officers standing around pointing and chatting, some tall and some short. They were the victors today, and it was obvious they were feeling very relaxed and confident. By this time, the large-scale mopping-up of resistance and search operations through the city had been concluded. In fact, before Ouyang Jue even entered the city, most of the foreign soldiers had already regrouped outside the walls. They were preparing to go and reinforce the Eight-Nation Alliance in the critical battle for Beijing.

As Ouyang Jue left the barbican and entered the city, it was worse than going down into hell itself. He could only imagine what hell would be like, but the massacre the old city had suffered was right in front of his eyes.

What was left of Tianjin lay before him.

This sight was followed by a blast of hot air hitting him right in the face. Day after day, the sun had blazed down without a drop of rain, and then for twenty-four hours at a stretch, tens of thousands of shells had lit fires from one end of the city to the other, raising the temperature within the walls to an appalling level. The ancient water-tanks in the four corners of the walls, which had stood there for five hundred years, were dry as a bone for the first time in their history.

It was impossible to walk down any of the main roads. A small number of foreign soldiers were still wandering around aimlessly, barging in wherever they liked, and if they thought something didn't feel quite right they would let fly with their guns. Stray bullets were pinging all over the place. On the field of battle, shooting quickly becomes completely unregulated. The line between life and death is a fine one and something over which you have no control.

Ouyang Jue was determined to return home alive. He decided to get off the main roads and walk through the lanes and alleyways over to the east part of the city, and then find a way to turn north and get back to Fushu Street where his family lived. He had grown up in the old city, and he could find his way around with his eyes shut – he'd never get lost. Like a field mouse, he knew every passageway and bolthole within his patch.

However, getting off the main roads didn't mean that he wasn't in danger any more. All over the city, you could still bump into foreign soldiers in their various uniforms; although there were not many of them, they were still very dangerous. At the far end of the narrow lane running next to the Xu family mansion, he saw a number of foreign soldiers shooting violently through a door opening. He didn't know what they were doing or who they could be shooting at. There were some tall marines up on top of the high northern city wall. It was so hot they had taken off most of their clothes, revealing pale reddish skin. They were standing up there, happily shooting into the city with a bang... bang... He couldn't even begin to imagine what had attracted their malevolent attention. When he was walking along the seemingly quiet alleyway towards Shen Family Lane behind the county yamen, he heard a burst of gunfire off to his right. He made haste to crouch down in a corner, only to see a foreign soldier chasing after a woman dressed in red who was running for her life. The soldier was shooting at her as he ran. For Tianjin people, red was a lucky colour to be worn on festive occasions – lots of girls wore red all the time. However, now the foreign soldiers thought that any woman dressed like that must be a Red Lantern, and the city was now littered with the corpses of girls in red, lying in pools of blood. The fresh blood dyed their dresses an even deeper shade of crimson.

Very few people were out and about in the city. Occasionally he might catch sight of one or two: carting off debris or moving something or other. Had everyone really run away, or were they hiding inside their houses with the doors barricaded? Ouyang Jue met a Chinese man holding up little flags of the allied countries, shouting as he made his way along the street. It seemed that there were still some people hiding in the city, holding fast or perhaps having nowhere else to go. Some shops along the road had their front doors kicked in; sometimes, you might see foreign soldiers inside ransacking the place. The antique shops that Ouyang Jue had so often frequented in the past were now empty, whatever had not been stolen had been smashed to bits. Foreigners wouldn't know a thing about Chinese antiques, but they must nevertheless have taken away these treasures quite happily as souvenirs. The looted shops looked like the corpses of bison after they have been eaten by lions.

Ouyang Jue saw no one as he walked from Gongyi Lane to Ding Family Lane and on to the Wenchang Belvedere. Here, the shelling had done much more damage – none of the houses had kept their roofs, and everything inside them had been burned. The whole place looked like row upon row of pitch-black brick kilns. You could imagine just how appalling yesterday's bombardment of this place must have been, with shells raining in from outside the walls for so many hours. Today, just looking at what was left, he felt frightened.

This was very close to his home.

He hadn't quite got back yet, but already he was developing a very bad feeling. He knew what the sense of foreboding that had engulfed him the other day meant. He almost didn't dare to go home.

When he entered Fushu Street, even at such a distance he could see that disaster had struck.

The huge and indomitable scholar tree, five hundred years old now, had gone. Its enormous trunk crushed the old house underneath it. He didn't know what had happened here, but he could see the dense smoke still rising up into the sky. A strong, pungent smell of burning hit him right in the face. There could be no doubt about it – the house had been destroyed. It had vanished like a ship lost beneath the waves.

He didn't know how he managed to walk the rest of the way home, what reserves of strength he called upon, nor could he be sure whether he'd run the whole way or whether he was so drained that he'd only managed to move one painful step at a time.

Before he'd even got back to the house, he could see that part of the big scholar tree had come down against the wall, and it had collapsed under the weight. A huge, leafy bough lay across the road. When he got to the front door, he saw that it had been broken open. The door itself was gone, and the opening wasn't barricaded.

What he saw when he went in was absolutely appalling.

The big elm-wood bench, which usually stood in the entranceway, was now in front of the screening wall opposite the door. There was a man sitting upright on the middle of the bench. His back was leaning against the screening wall; his head wrapped in red cloth, his hands gripped tight to the handle of a hatchet, and his eyes open wide. Who was this man? At a time like this, how could he be on guard by the door like that? A second glance told him – it was Zhang Yi! Before he called out to him, he realised that the man was dead. His chest was riddled with bullet holes, and his massive feet were soaking in a pool of blood. The carved screening wall behind him, its smoothly-polished slabs put together seamlessly, had been shot to pieces. Just from the density of the bullet holes pockmarking the screening wall, he could see just how trigger-happy the soldiers that broke in here must have been.

He hurried in, walked round the screening wall, and ran along the corridor leading to the courtyard where his father lived until he got to the entrance and saw what lay ahead… then he knew that the worst had happened. Not only had the foreigners' shelling destroyed all the buildings here, but it had also blown up the huge old tree. Both the huge crown and the thick trunk had been blasted to pieces, crushing the ruined house below – if his father had been in his rooms when that came down, he would have been doomed! He called out to his father again and again, but he couldn't force his way into the courtyard. The fallen old scholar tree and the remains of the ancient house were heaped up there. Through a gap in the debris, he could see his father's purple bamboo walking stick lying abandoned on the ground.

If his father had run away before any of this started, why was his walking stick still there? Would he have gone anywhere? How about Zun and his wife? And Shuxian?

He ran to the middle courtyard where his elder brother lived. Here, only the side rooms had been destroyed by exploding shells; the main residential block had not collapsed. Half of the courtyard was filled with branches and leaves from the fallen tree. When the tree toppled over, the momentum must have been enormous. Some of the denser branches had broken through the shuttered windows, and these boughs had forced their way into the house.

Ouyang Jue ran into his elder brother's bedroom and called his name twice. No one answered. The whole place was in a disarray – it had obviously been ransacked, but there was no sign of anyone having been killed there. Where could his brother and sister-in-law have gone? Were the volunteers he'd talked to yesterday outside the city, when he bumped into them in that little village as they were transporting shells to the foreign troops, actually right: had they run away already? If they'd really gone, his elder brother would have insisted on their father going with them. So what about Shuxian? Had Shuxian left too? If the whole family had gone, why had Zhang Yi fought to the death to stop anyone going through the front door?

He turned around and raced to his own rooms.

As soon as he entered the door, he saw the most dreadful scene.

She was not inside the house; everything had happened out in the courtyard. His rooms had not been destroyed in the shelling, but the courtyard was filled with the vast quantities of branches and leaves that had scattered when the big scholar tree fell. Torn-off flowers and leaves were spread all over the ground. Shuxian had died on the porch in front of the house. She was lying there, her dress ripped to shreds, leaving her legs and part of her lower body naked. She'd killed herself by beating her brains out against one of the pillars of the porch; the blood had trickled down the pillar from head-height. She had killed herself rather than live with the humiliations inflicted upon her.

There was more blood beside the well in the courtyard. Someone had jumped down it, head first – again, this person was naked from the waist down. Judging from the bound feet, it had to be Mrs Jiang.

Ouyang Jue fell to the ground.

Right at that moment, he felt he might as well be dead; he had no idea what to do next. He wandered aimlessly around in the courtyard, turning a half circle there; then he went into the house, walked another half circle in their bedroom and came out again; afterwards, he drifted over to his study. He'd spent a good part of each day there for over a decade, but now it seemed to have nothing to do with him. It was only when he caught sight of the three porcelain jars sitting on his desk, each one of them filled with melon seeds, that all of a sudden he came to his senses...

Now, in a flash, he was back in the real world; he had returned to the happy family life he'd known before, and he could see again that loving face and familiar voice. She'd cracked melon seeds for him, poured him tea, chatted to him about poetry and painting, and made sure his favourite foods and clothes were ready for him. She'd been very well-educated, she was so sweet-natured and kind, so good to everyone, so modest and restrained. She was undemanding, uncontentious – she had never done anything to hurt any other living creature, so why had she suffered such a terrible fate, worse than being confined to the eighteen pits of hell? Why should she have had to suffer being gang-raped and abused by those animals? When he thought about what had happened here, it was driving him mad! He began to cry, first weeping in silence and then wailing in misery at the top of his voice… She had died because she was waiting for him; she had suffered for his sake. Compared with either himself or Xénia, his wife was a completely innocent party. He felt sad for her. He was pained and angry on her behalf. He hated himself and felt a terrible regret for the way he'd treated her, but he knew that even if he killed himself, it would not help in the slightest.

He never knew how long it took for him to get up and drag his desk out of the study, put it in the middle of the courtyard, pick up Shuxian and lay her out flat, and then go and collect a clean sheet to cover her after carefully arranging her hair. After death, her eyes had remained fixed open with a frightened and resentful expression. Now, he closed her eyes gently, so that she could rest as peacefully as she normally did.

Afterwards, he collected the porcelain jars of melon seeds from his study and sprinkled them over her body like flower-petals until it looked as if the blossoms of the scholar tree had covered her.

He then carried out his paintings, poetry manuscripts, articles, calligraphy paper and brushes, as well as the books that filled his rooms, stacking them neatly all around her. He filled the white stone well-head in the middle of the courtyard with more paper and silks, as well as branches from the scholar tree.

Once that was done, he set fire to it all.

He collapsed over to one side, waiting for the flames to start to burn, and watched the fire and smoke engulf his wife's body. Afterwards, the fire spread along the corridor, burning the rooms on all four sides, as well as the thick and vigorous trunk of the old scholar tree that had quietly sheltered the house for hundreds of years before it fell. When it was burning briskly with loud crackling noises, he walked out of the courtyard, out of the house, onto the street and all the way out beyond the walls – he never once looked back.

He didn't know where his brother and sister-in-law were, whether they had escaped or whether they had already been killed. He only knew that his father must have died when the house collapsed on top of him. He was quite sure that his father would never have left Shuxian behind on her own; their loyal servitor Zhang Yi had been killed at the gate trying to protect them.

But right now he simply didn't care any more.

On Fushu Street, the fire was burning ever more fiercely. The flames leaping from the huge ancient tree were shooting up twenty metres or more as it burned – they could be seen halfway across the city. All the members of the local fire-brigade had run away, so there was no one to put out the flames: it just had to burn itself out. The thick smoke filled with sadness darkened the summer sky above the old city.

This was the worst of the fires that burned when Tianjin fell.

CHAPTER 16

A commander from the Eight-Nation Alliance surveying the fighting from an artillery position

WHEN OUYANG JUE left the city, he didn't think about where he was going, nor did he make the slightest effort to avoid running into danger. He had seen too much, experienced too much... he simply didn't care what happened to him any more. A stray bullet carried away one part of his ear, but he didn't even notice. He let the blood flow, dripping down onto his shoulder, dying the collar of his shirt red.

In fact, by this time, the city had already descended into chaos. Most of the defeated Boxers had abandoned the city, throwing away their symbolic turbans as they fled, mingling with the ordinary refugees. Those who tried to fight back were killed – the final victims of the slaughter unleashed by the foreign troops. The survivors from the Qing garrison had found refuge among the villages west of the city, such as Yangliuqing, Jinghai, Duliu and Beicang; though some had raced back to Beijing to rescue the emperor and the rest of the imperial family. The situation in the capital was critical – having crushed Tianjin, a significant number of troops from the Eight-Nation Alliance was advancing along the railway line, bursting with confidence. They were going to root out the barbarians' rat's nest. Supposedly, the Dowager Empress Cixi had already fled westwards with the emperor and empress. Some officers in the Qing Army realised that the tide was turning against them, so they began to turn their guns against the Boxers as they scattered.

The situation in Tianjin now descended into utter lawlessness.

As the foreign soldiers withdrew, the Chinese Christians, who had suffered so much before, re-emerged, bent on vengeance, and the local criminals were also out and about, setting fires and stealing things. All the abandoned houses and shops in this empty city were open and undefended: anyone could just walk straight in. These people were getting into fights – even killing each other – over their loot. There were plenty of corpses floating in the moat outside the city; the foreigners only collected their own dead, and they'd hired coolies from the city to use the leaves of doors as stretchers to carry them away. The corpses of Boxers and refugees were not being dealt with, and the weather was appallingly hot, so the day after the massacre they were already starting to stink.

People were absolutely desperate for food and water. By the gates to the city, a few traders were selling cakes and biscuits, but you had to be able to pay in Guangxu-era silver ingots or in jewellery.

However, none of this had anything to do with him.

When Ouyang Jue passed through the Daying Gate, he ran straight into the foreign soldiers on guard there, but no one stopped him or questioned him. Looking at his eyes, they could see that he was out of his mind. At that time, there were many such deeply traumatised people wandering around inside and outside the city.

He walked straight towards the Foreign Concession, through the wilderness, and on through some small battlefields and temporary encampments. There were no living people here, just the dead. Swords, guns and flags lay on the ground wherever they had fallen, and the bodies were those of members of the Militia of Righteous Harmony and the Qing Army, along with the occasional foreigner.

He picked up a sword from the ground. When he raised it, there was a clear flame of hatred in his eyes.

He kept on walking straight ahead.

In front of him, out on the open plain, he could see many black crows and a couple of dogs. He couldn't see whether they were starving dogs or wolves. At that time, the wilderness outside Tianjin stretched uninterrupted all the way to Manchuria, and that meant wolves did occasionally make their way here.

The battlefield has always offered a feast for creatures of this kind. As soon as he approached, they scattered in all directions and stopped not far away to stare at him. He could see that there were some human remains lying out on the plain, splashed with bright red blood; the places where they had been bitten by the animals showed fresh and raw. Suddenly, a headless body appeared in his field of vision. The man must have had his head blown off by a shell. He noticed that headless corpse had a very strange pistol clasped in one hand. The barrel was unusually long, and it seemed familiar to him. He remembered something Xénia had told him: she said that her father liked this kind of long-barrelled pistol very much because it could shoot great distances. She also said she didn't like weapons either.

Ouyang Jue immediately went over to inspect the torso of the corpse. He was apparently looking for something – and he found it. Hanging from the belt was another bronze tube, but this time it was a telescope. He knew it only too well!

That telescope was something that once meant the world to him, but now… he was quite simply indifferent.

This man was Xénia's father. He must have been one of the commanders of the Allied Army's attack on Tianjin.

Just as he raised the sword in his hand, he heard a growling sound beside him. When he looked around, not far from the body, there was a poodle – it was their brown curly-haired poodle! The dog was guarding its master.

After that first growl, it didn't make another sound and lay there motionless, just like on that day out at the little white house when he'd come down the stairs from the attic room to discover it. The dog seemed to know him; there was a soft look in its eyes as it watched him quietly.

He looked at it for a moment. He did nothing but just walked away.

When he approached the Foreign Concession, a shot rang out from a hillock in front of him. Someone was shouting at Ouyang Jue in a foreign language. He saw that on top of the hill there were some earthworks built with sandbags: he had arrived at the front lines of the Foreign Concession's defences. He paused for a moment then raised his sword and walked straight ahead without any hesitation. They opened fire, and the bullets went whistling past him. He kept on walking with his sword held high, and a second volley of bullets was fired, but he didn't even notice whereabouts he had been shot.

He suddenly saw that there was a strange thing standing right on the horizon, over to the left behind the defensive line. It was tiny and a very long way away – but he knew immediately that it was that little white house. At that moment, the setting sun slanted across from the west across the open plain, shining on the small building. In the strong evening light, it stood all alone, the darkening Foreign Concession forming a grey backdrop behind it. The building shone golden-red in the light, so brightly, like a tombstone far, far away in the wilderness. However, no matter how many memories had once been held within this strange place, none of it meant anything to him now.

He carried on walking straight forward.

There was a shout from opposite, and then another intense burst of gunfire.

ABOUT THE AUTHOR

Born in Tianjin in 1942, Feng Jicai is a contemporary author, artist and cultural scholar who rose to prominence as a pioneer of China's Scar Literature movement that emerged after the Cultural Revolution. He has published almost a hundred literary works in China and more than forty internationally. He is proficient in both Chinese and Western artistic techniques, and his artwork has been exhibited in China, Japan, the US, Singapore and Austria. He has had a major influence on contemporary Chinese society with his work on the Project to Save Chinese Folk Cultural Heritages and his roles as honorary member of the Literature and Arts Association, honorary president of the China Folk Literature and Art Association and adviser to the State Council, among others. He is also dean, professor and PhD supervisor at the Feng Jicai Institute of Literature and Art, Tianjin University.

ABOUT THE TRANSLATOR

Olivia Milburn is professor of Chinese language and literature at Seoul National University. She completed her first degree in Chinese at St Hilda's College, University of Oxford, a master's in Oriental studies at Downing College, University of Cambridge, and a doctorate in classical Chinese at the School of Oriental and African Studies, University of London. She has authored several books including *Cherishing Antiquity: The Cultural Construction of an Ancient Chinese Kingdom*, *The Spring and Autumn Annals of Master Yan* and *Urbanization in Early and Medieval China: Gazetteers for the City of Suzhou*. In collaboration with Christopher Payne, she has translated two spy novels by Mai Jia, including the bestselling *Decoded*, from Chinese to English. In 2018, Milburn's translation work was recognised by the Chinese government with a Special Book Award of China, which honours contributions to bridging cultures and fostering understanding.

About **Sino**ist Books

We hope Jue and Xénia's doomed romance stirred you.

SINOIST BOOKS brings the best of Chinese fiction to English-speaking readers. We aim to create a greater understanding of Chinese culture and society, and provide an outlet for the ideas and creativity of the country's most talented authors.

To let us know what you thought of this book, or to learn more about the diverse range of exciting Chinese fiction in translation we publish, find us online. If you're as passionate about Chinese literature as we are, then we'd love to hear your thoughts!

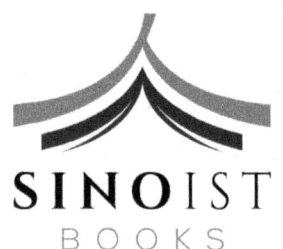

sinoistbooks.com
@sinoistbooks